The Kingdom of God:
A Biblical Perspective

By Chad Sychtysz

© 2025 Spiritbuilding Publishers.
All rights reserved. No part of this book may be reproduced in any form without the written permission of the publisher.

Published by
Spiritbuilding Publishers
9700 Ferry Road, Waynesville, Ohio 45068

THE KINGDOM OF GOD
A Biblical Perspective
By Chad Sychtysz

ISBN: 978-1-964-80544-3

Cover Design by Caitlyn Cline

Spiritbuilding
PUBLISHERS

spiritbuilding.com

Table of Contents

Introduction 1
Part 1   **The Kingdom That Jesus Preached** 7
Chapter 1   God's Kingdom Has Always Been 8
Chapter 2   Development of God's Kingdom in the Bible 17
Chapter 3   The Nature of the Kingdom 28
Chapter 4   The Sons of the Kingdom 37
Part 2   **The Kingdom and Salvation** 51
Chapter 5   The Purpose of Christ's Rule over the Kingdom 52
Chapter 6   Kingdom and Salvation: Two Side of the Same Coin 62
Chapter 7   The Kingdom and the Church 72
Chapter 8   Mount Zion and New Jerusalem 83
Chapter 9   The Present and Future Kingdom 92
Chapter 10   A New World Order 105
Part 3   **Citizenship in the Kingdom** 119
Chapter 11   The Blessedness of the Kingdom 120
Chapter 12   The Kingdom of Love, Light, and Truth 130
Chapter 13   Seeking First the Kingdom 142
Chapter 14   Working in the Kingdom 152
Chapter 15   Inheriting the Kingdom 160
Sources Used 169
Endnotes 171

Unless otherwise noted, Scripture taken from the
NEW AMERICAN STANDARD BIBLE®.
Copyright © 1960, 1962, 1963, 1968, 1971, 1972, 1973, 1975, 1977, 1995
by The Lockman Foundation. Used by permission.

The author can be contacted at chad@booksbychad.com.

Introduction to
The Kingdom of God:
A Biblical Perspective

Now after John [the Baptist] had been taken into custody, Jesus came into Galilee, preaching the gospel of God, and saying, "The time is fulfilled, and the kingdom of God is at hand; repent and believe in the gospel" (Mark 1:14–15).

This electric proclamation is near the beginning of Mark's gospel, which chronologically was likely the first of the four gospels of the New Testament (NT). You can almost hear the people talking excited amongst themselves: "This Man—the miracle-worker—is talking about the long-awaited kingdom of God! What we have waited for through centuries of anguished anticipation is about to happen! Do you know what this means? Our freedom is near"—and some, "We will finally be released from our heathen oppressors!"

Jesus knew His countrymen would react this way. He was not born into a calm world of stagnant, sleepy religious contentment. Quite the opposite: He deliberately entered a world of tense expectations, religious confusion, and brooding for centuries over what one Gentile ruler after another had imposed upon them. Judea had been under Roman occupation for one hundred years. Even when treated with partiality over other nations in the Roman Empire, Jews—*God's people*—hotly resented being subject to pagan rulers.[1]

Yet, Jesus was also not the only one who had made such a statement. The NT itself records a man named Theudas who tried to incite an insurrection against the Roman military presence in Judea and amassed some four hundred followers.[2] After he was killed, the entire plan evaporated. Later, an insurrectionist named Judas of Galilee during the time when Jesus was born arose, but he also was killed and his movement fizzled (Acts 5:36–37).[3] Even *after* Jesus died, others would claim to be "the Messiah"—in essence, the Jews' long-awaited deliverer-king—but they would all be impostors (Mat. 24:4–5).

But Jesus was no impostor—someone who made specious claims without stunning support. And He was no upstart revolutionary—the head of an otherwise hopeless band of malcontents. Instead, Jesus came speaking of things no one else had ever talked about, and with unprecedented authority. He came fulfilling one Old Testament (OT) prophecy after another. He came healing, forgiving, overcoming the natural elements, and exorcising demons. He came with irrefutable evidence that He was, indeed, not another angry, starry-eyed, and over-ambitious Jew, but Someone who confounded the self-serving Jewish teachers on their own turf, feeding thousands of people from a sparse amount of food, walking on water, calming storms, and even *raising the dead.*

In other words, Jesus entered a world pregnant with anticipation for relief from Roman oppression, redemption from centuries of their own bad decisions, anxious to reclaim the glory days of King David and King Solomon and simply were "distressed and dispirited like sheep without a shepherd" (Mat. 9:36). And the "kingdom of God" was at the center of all of this.

The arrival of the kingdom of God would usher in an age of earthly glory in which Israel would once again be the crowning jewel of the world—geographically, politically, and religiously. The nation of Israel would be purified of all its bad elements; all its enemies would be destroyed or forced to submit to Israel and its King. A Davidic King/Messiah would be the ruler and judge of the entire world; even the physical world would be made glorious.[4] Like the prophet Isaiah promised centuries ago (Isa. 60:1-7), the nations would stream to Jerusalem with their praise, their rejoicing, and their wealth.[5]

This is what many of the Jews thought, anyway. The reality was far better than this, but they were stuck in preconceived perceptions of the kingdom of God, preventing them from seeing Jesus for who and what He really was. The Jews desperately wanted an earthly king, an earthly kingdom, and triumph over earthly oppressors. They assumed that, simply because they *were* Jews, they would automatically be part of this glorious kingdom. Therefore, they thought, they would be recipients of all this power, success, and glory.

This is not much different than where many Christians are today: not having an accurate understanding of God's kingdom, they are wishing for something that God did not say or are interpreting what He *did* say because of preconceived expectations. Many assume that, simply because they are *called* "Christians," they automatically are (or will be) part of this Davidic-styled kingdom. "Nominalism," in which name or terminology is solely what binds people together, "is the curse of modern western Christianity."[6]

The topic of the kingdom of God is, admittedly, not an easy one to explain. On the surface, it is a simple concept. Yet the more one digs into biblical teachings on this, it becomes a subject that involves the entire Bible and has a depth that no one can seem to explain or understand completely. It is not necessary, however, to learn everything there is to know about the kingdom of God before having a practical understanding of it and a great appreciation for God's work in the human world.

While the kingdom of God is the centerpiece of God's plan of redemption, Jesus Christ is the centerpiece of the kingdom, and therefore He is in the middle of everything. He is the world's Redeemer, and God's kingdom is what makes this redemption possible. If there was no kingdom (in the way Jesus spoke of it), then there could be no Redeemer—and there could be no forgiveness of our sins, no church of God's people, and no promise of heaven. All this is in the background of what Jesus was proclaiming to the Jews and is the reason for His earthly ministry among them.

The amount of attention to which Jesus gives the kingdom of God is significant. Proportionately, it is one of the most frequent topics of His teachings. The so-called "sermon on the mount" (Mat. 5–7) is all about getting one's heart prepared to enter the kingdom. The many kingdom parables are among the most revealing explanations that we have about the nature of the kingdom. From the beginning of His ministry (as cited earlier in Mark 1:14–15) to the very end of His life (in His conversation with Pilate in John 18:33–37), the kingdom was on Jesus' mind. Even after His resurrection, He appeared to His apostles "speaking of the things concerning the kingdom of God" (Acts 1:3).

Jesus' kingdom teaching was not merely "Be good people; love, forgive, serve, etc." These are God's moral expectations of His people, to be sure, but the kingdom is not merely moralistic.[7] He also talked about power, authority, and the ability to render heavenly decisions, but He did not define the kingdom merely by power and authority. He also talked about His kingly role as a righteous Judge—One who can and will render divine decisions concerning people. These decisions will affect, He said, the Jewish nation (Luke 19:11–27), those who claim to identify with Him (Mat. 25:31–46), and the entirety of humankind (John 5:25–29; see also 2 Cor. 5:10). But the purpose of the kingdom of God is not merely to give Christ the authority to judge people.

The kingdom's message—its purpose, its function, and the core of Jesus' preaching about it—is all about *saving human souls*. These other things (morality, authority, future judgments, etc.) are all part of this great plan, but the *reason* for the plan is to offer spiritual redemption to those lost in sin—and *all* of us, apart from divine grace, are lost in sin. Mercy, grace, forgiveness, walking in God's light, and heavenly promises are all made possible because of the One whom God has crowned as King over all His kingdom. This is the "eternal purpose which He carried out in Christ Jesus our Lord" (Eph. 3:11), and Jesus has proven Himself to be altogether worthy of fulfilling this grand purpose.

I do not have all the answers about the kingdom of God. Despite my best efforts put forth in this book, you will likely still have questions about the kingdom that either I did not or cannot answer. You should know, too, that while I am providing a biblical perspective and practical explanation of the kingdom, there are far more complex investigations into it. These writings are usually philosophical, written in difficult seminary language, and ultimately (in my opinion) do not offer much to Christians. (I have read several of these books; they are usually dense, wordy, and exhausting.) Here's an example:

> [The kingdom of God is] *"Creationally engaged, universally focused, and eschatologically oriented, the kingdom of God is a transcendent sphere of reality that conspires with a community of human image-bearers in the task of restoring creation to the worship of the one true creator God."*[8]

The objective of this book you are reading is not to overwhelm you with religious philosophy, nor to impress you with my vocabulary. In my strong opinion, based upon decades of working with Christians, people need understandable language and straightforward answers. They need to learn biblical concepts, to be sure, but they also need to know how to implement those concepts in their everyday walk with God.

Jesus did not tell us everything there is to know about the kingdom of God, nor did His apostles. For us to know everything about God's kingdom, we would have to know everything about God, His Spirit, and Jesus Himself—information that exceeds our comprehension. But what we *do* know—what we *have* been told—is sufficient for us to conduct ourselves as citizens *of* God's kingdom.

Thirty-five hundred years ago, Moses said, "The secret things belong to the LORD our God, but the things revealed belong to us and to our sons forever, that we may observe all the words of this law" (Deut. 29:29). While the law then was the Law of Moses, and *our* law is the "law of Christ" (Gal. 6:2), the principle remains timeless and unchanged. God tells us what we *need* to know—no more, and no less. It is this information that we are to believe, teach, and practice.

Two thousand years ago, Jesus preached what is as relevant today as it was then: "repent and believe in the gospel" (Mark 1:15). Repenting, believing, and (necessarily implied) *living* the gospel of the kingdom is what *citizens* of the kingdom *do*. This is where God wants us; this is what Jesus lived and died for; and this serves your best interest. It is worth our time and energy to dive into this fantastic subject in anticipation of where it leads us: into the real, visible, and glorious presence of the King.

Part One:

The Kingdom That Jesus Preached

Chapter One

God's Kingdom Has Always Been

It might appear that when Jesus preached about it, the kingdom of God had never previously existed. This implies that He was preaching something new, something that was about to come into existence, and that this new existence was "at hand [or, near]" (Mark 1:15). The answer to this is both *no* and *yes* all at once.

God has always been the King over all that exists, whether in the physical and visible realm or in the spiritual and invisible realm.[9] He could not have been the Creator of the physical world unless He had authority and ability to do so. If His authority had been derived from a yet higher authority, then He is not *the* King but is, at best, *a* King. But we know of no other authority; there is no evidence for another authority; and we never see God, in anything He says or does, asking permission of or seeking to conform to this authority. In fact, God Himself says, "Is there any God besides Me, or is there any other Rock? I know of none" (Isa. 44:8).[10] Moses concurs:

> To you it was shown that you might know that the Lord, He is God; there is no other besides Him. … Know therefore today, and take it to your heart, that the Lord, He is God in heaven above and on the earth below; there is no other. (Deut. 4:35, 39)[11]

This means, too, that He has always had all authority over all that exists—and authority is a primary subject when dealing with God and His kingdom. The psalmists recognized God's kingship and kingdom:

- "For the kingdom is the Lord's and He rules over the nations" (Psalm 22:28).
- "Your throne, O God, is forever and ever; a scepter of uprightness is the scepter of Your kingdom" (Psalm 45:6).

- ❑ "Sing praises to God, sing praises; sing praises to our King, sing praises" (Psalm 47:6).
- ❑ "Righteousness and justice are the foundation of Your throne; lovingkindness and truth go before You. ... For our shield belongs to the LORD, and our king to the Holy One of Israel" (Psalm 89:14, 18).
- ❑ "Your kingdom is an everlasting kingdom, and Your dominion endures throughout all generations" (Psalm 145:13).

Even Darius, king of Babylon in the Persian Empire, recognized this after he discovered that God rescued Daniel from the lion's den: "I make a decree that in all the dominion of my kingdom men are to fear and tremble before the God of Daniel; for He is the living God and enduring forever, and His kingdom is one which will not be destroyed, and His dominion will be forever" (Dan. 6:26).

There is no question that God is the King over all that exists. Even Christ, though He is the Son of God, recognizes this and submits to His Father's kingship. Paul wrote, "But I want you to understand that Christ is the head of every man, and the man is the head of a woman, and God is the head of Christ" (1 Cor. 11:3). When God made His Son (Christ) the King over His kingdom, He Himself was exempted from His Son's oversight (1 Cor. 15:27–28). It cannot be that God the King would be ruled by His Son. When God made His Son King, He did not relinquish His own kingship but simply delegated all His authority to His Son.

Since Christ submits to God's authority, then everything under *Christ's* authority submits by default to this authority. This is not a new thing (having only begun when Christ took the throne) but has always been. Christ has always *been* the Son of God, and He has created all that has *been* created.[12]

Having brought human life into existence (Gen. 1:27, 2:7, and 2:18–23), God established dominance, authority, and power—in essence, kingship—over all human life. (The same can be said of *all* living things on earth and in the spiritual realm.) He instructed His human creation

(Adam) to exercise authority over all the earth, having put "all things [on earth] in subjection under his [man's] feet" (Psalm 8:5–6, Heb. 2:7–8).

God could not have given life to Man (both male and female human beings—see Gen. 5:2) unless He had the authority and ability to do so. He could not have ordered Man to subdue the earth unless He already had authority over all the earth. This authority, and the ability to exercise it in the form of specific actions, establishes His authority and defines Him as King.

Likewise, we know that God promised David, king of Israel, an eternal throne (2 Sam. 7:12–16). This meant that David himself would prefigure a transcendent "David" that would take His seat on a far greater and more powerful throne than King David could have ever imagined. The takeaway here, for the time being, is that God could not have promised David an eternal throne (in essence, a King that came through his lineage whose kingdom would supersede all other kingdoms) unless He had the *authority* and *ability* to make this happen.

God cannot promise a mortal man that his would become an eternal kingdom unless God first had His own eternal kingdom. If there were another, greater king to whom God had to answer or give allegiance, He could never have made this promise without consulting with and gaining permission of this other being. But we see nowhere—as in *nowhere*—in all the Bible that even remotely suggests that there exists a greater power than God. In fact, the very fact that God *is* God requires that there be no higher power than Himself.[13]

It is conspicuous, too, that God never asked permission of anyone to reign over all the earth and over all the kingdoms of men. He speaks from a position of inherent authority, not granted authority. Even today, God rules over all humanity but does not ask (or need) permission to do this. He does not need our consent; we cannot deny or ignore His rule with impunity. His authority already exceeds that of everything that He has created; these are all inferior to Him.

As the source of all authority, creative power, salvation, truth, goodness, and life itself, God must be King over all realms that exist. This includes both the physical realm (the natural universe as well as the realm of human life) and the spiritual realm (that which is invisible to human sight).

Even as king over Israel, David understood that God was still the King over the entire world (2 Chron. 29:9–12). God did not step aside or abdicate His kingship to allow Israel to have its own king; instead, Israel's king was a human representative of God's justice in the land, as the high priest was a representative of His holiness among His people.

The Bible repeatedly, consistently, and unapologetically depicts God the Father as the highest authority that exists, period. This is important since there is no greater source of written authority than the Bible concerning the spiritual realm and the origin of the physical world. No person can know the origin of the world unless Scripture revealed this information to *all humankind*. Science points to what exists and how it functions; it cannot explain the beginning *of* existence, or even how natural laws and scientific processes came to be.

The question, then, is not whether God is the King over all that exists. The real question is: what does it mean that God has a kingdom? And then, what is the activity of this kingdom?

King and Kingdom: A "king," both historically and by definition, is a ruler, overseer, lawmaker, and (often indirectly) law enforcer. He is the highest authority in whatever realm he oversees. There can be lesser kings over parts of his kingdom, and this is not contradictory. For example, Christ has the royal title of "King of kings, and Lord of lords" (Rev. 19:16), indicating that all other kings (or lords) and their kingdoms do in fact exist but are subordinate to Him and His kingdom (see also Eph. 1:20–21 and Col. 1:15–16).

"Kingdom" is a compound word that means, quite literally, "the domain of the king." Whatever a king controls, manages, and exercises royal authority over is his domain. Whatever and whoever is in this domain answers to the king. (The king may empower lesser authorities to govern citizens and affairs of state, but *he* remains the highest authority.) A domain involves both the king's legal superiority *and* positional authority (over territory, people, governments, courts, etc.). There is no higher legal authority or position.

> The term "kingdom" is in English somewhat ambiguous, but it naturally suggests a territory or community governed by a king. The Greek term *basileia* which it translates is also ambiguous. But there can be no doubt that the expression before us [i.e., "kingdom of heaven"] represents an Aramaic phrase well established in Jewish usage, "the Malkuth of Heaven." Malkuth...is properly an abstract noun, meaning "kingship," "kingly rule," "reign," or "sovereignty." The expression "the malkuth of God" connotes the fact that God reigns as King.[14]

> The primary meaning of both the Hebrew word *malkuth* in the Old Testament and of the Greek work *basileia* ["kingdom"] in the New Testament is the rank, authority and sovereignty exercised by a king. A *basileia* may indeed be a realm over which a sovereign exercises his authority; and it may be the people who belong to that realm and over whom authority is exercised; but these are secondary and derived meanings. First of all, a kingdom is the authority to rule, the sovereignty of the king.[15]

We are looking at this through the lens of how people have viewed kings for most of human history. Our American democratic system, with its three branches of government and bicameral i.e., two-house) Congress does not help us to understand the concept of a king. Our president is not the king; he answers to the Constitution, Congress, and the American people. In a monarchical system, there is one king who rules over all people and lands within his realm. "Monarch" means "one ruler [or overseer]," and while monarchy can take different forms (benevolent ruler, military ruler, tyrant, despot, etc.), it still means that one person oversees everything within his kingdom (or royal domain).

Theoretically, a monarch can make laws by his own authority. This was the case with the Babylonian king Nebuchadnezzar, who, by his own personal decrees, made laws and declared edicts that required no one else's advisement, permission, or confirmation. (This is particularly evident in Dan. 1 – 3.) Later, the Persian emperors occupied the highest *position* in the land but were not the greatest *legal authority* in the land. It was the "law of the Medes and Persians" (Dan. 6:8, etc.) which had that role. For what it is worth, in our American government our Constitution serves in this same role: there is no single person who rules over the United States, but our Constitution is the law of the land.

In Israel's early national history, when it journeyed out of Egypt, through the wilderness for forty years and then into Canaan, God was their King. Initially, they had no human king to rule over them, only judges or God-appointed deliverers. This describes a theocracy, a God-governed nation (from *theos* [God] + *kratos* [power]). God ruled over the people through His judges, His law, His priests (which His law ordained), and His prophets. God oversaw not only all religious aspects of Israel but also all social, political, and even economic aspects as well. God rewarded obedience with great prosperity; God repaid disobedience—and especially idolatry—with great punishment (consider Deut. 28:1–62 regarding these thoughts).

God's rule over Israel did not fully define His kingdom, however. He simultaneously ruled over all the heathen nations as well (even though He did not have a covenant relationship with them). This was why He leveled judgments against these nations for their flagrant and persistent infidelity to God's covenant. And He ruled over the entire physical universe as well (Psalm 8:3, Isa. 40:26, Jer. 31:35, etc.).

In other words, the kingdom of Israel (and later, of Judah) did not represent, equal, or ever exercise power over God's kingdom since He reigned over all that came to exist. Whatever God made "In the beginning" (Gen. 1:1) was forever under His authority. He was (and is) King over all living beings, principalities, and worlds.

The Kings of Israel: Ultimately, the Israelites asked for a human king so they could be like all the other nations (since there was no other nation in which a human-conceived god ruled over and communicated with it).[16] God said to Samuel, the judge over Israel at that time, "Listen to the voice of the people in regard to all that they say to you, for they have not rejected you, but they have rejected Me from being king over them" (1 Sam. 8:7). The prophet Isaiah later thought that he was a dead man when God appeared to him in a vision: "Woe is me, for I am ruined! Because I am a man of unclean lips, and I live among a people of unclean lips; for my eyes have seen the King, the LORD of hosts" (Isa. 6:5).

Israel's rejection of God's kingship, either by asking for a human king or through their indulgence in idolatry, did not rob God of His kingly rule or the power or extent of His kingdom. It just meant that God's relationship with Israel would be forever changed. "The King is no less King because His citizens have rebelled. His royal sovereignty hasn't been overthrown nor has God abdicated."[17]

Israel's rejection of God's kingship paved the way for its headlong rush into idolatry and paganism, but it did not have to be this way. God anointed David and Solomon, for example, as kings to rule over His people and promised both men great rewards if they remained faithful to Him (1 Kings 9:1–9). David, through trial and error, honored God's promise; Solomon did not.

Even when human kings reigned over Israel (and Judah), God's law, priests, and prophets did not cease to exert great spiritual (and sometimes practical) influence over the people. Righteous Israelites still honored God's law (see Psalm 119, for example); God's faithful priests continued to offer holy sacrifices; and God's prophets continued to condemn all forms of idolatry but also strongly encourage the people to walk with integrity.

We can look at this as the effect and influence of God's kingdom—not the individual kingdoms of men, but God's transcendent heavenly kingdom that governed and maintained control over the entire human race as well as the physical realm. Whenever men walked with God, they walked in agreement with God's kingdom; those who sought God as *their* King embodied His kingdom teachings, virtues, and values.

This thought affects how we see Jesus' own teaching on the kingdom of God in His ministry. He taught that those who were *of* God's kingdom would be those who *embraced, embodied,* and *conformed* to the King (Jesus). "An analysis of 119 passages in the New Testament where the expression 'Kingdom' occurs, shows that it means the rule of God; which was manifested in and through Christ; is apparent in 'the Church'; gradually develops amidst hindrances; is triumphant at the second coming of Christ ('the end'); and, finally, perfected in the world to come."[18]

Summary Thoughts: God's kingdom did not begin when Jesus began to reign over it but has always existed. God could not have created the world unless He had kingly authority to do so, and whatever He did create inherently became part of His kingdom. He could not have made promises about David or Jesus unless He had kingly authority to do so. Only in this overarching sense, God's kingdom—the entire realm of Creation—does not include only those who submit to His authority but to all whom He has brought into existence. His kingship is the highest position that exists; no one can usurp, supersede, or opt out of His oversight. He was King over Israel when they were faithful as well as when they were unfaithful; He was King over all the nations, regardless of their response to Him.

Israel did ask for a human king to reign over them, and God permitted this (with stipulations). Israel could have done well with this arrangement—and did do well under certain kings—but they gradually pulled away from God and became steeped in idolatry. When God sent the two nations (Israel and Judah) into exile, this did cure them of idolatry but did not repair their kingdom or fulfill the kingdom promises that God made through their prophets. Human kingdoms would all eventually disappear, but the kingdom of God would be revealed to the world through the teachings, miracles, and virtues of His Son, Jesus Christ.

We have much to say about this in time.

Chapter Two

Development of God's Kingdom in the Bible

As one's study of the Bible (and especially the OT) deepens, the more conspicuous God's kingdom becomes. One might say that the entire Bible is really about the kingdom of God, and it presents this kingdom in two distinct phases. **First**, there is the anticipation of its revelation to humankind through the kingship of God's Son. **Second**, there is the Son's rule over God's kingdom in which He builds His church and spreads the influence of kingdom-teaching throughout the world.

The kingdom of Israel is essential in the gradual revelation of the kingdom of God. This does not mean that Israel's kingdom becomes God's kingdom: one is a kingdom of men, the other is of God; one is of this world, the other is not of this world. However, there is a link between the two kingdoms: one (Israel's) foreshadows the other (God's), not in power or moral quality but in concept and basic design.

The kingdom of God is revealed through Israel—the nation, kings, priests, Law, and temple. These elements are embedded in God's kingdom, though in a spiritual context. The nation represents the whole of Creation; kings of Israel, the King of all Creation; Levitical priests, the High Priest of the Kingdom; the Law of Moses, the law of God's kingdom; and the temple, God's heavenly tabernacle that presides over all Creation.

The only physical element common between the two kingdoms is a blood offering in atoning for sin. This was carried out as a "type" prophecy through animal sacrifices in the Law of Moses, but Christ has fulfilled that prophecy both for the Law and what God requires for entrance into the kingdom of God. (A "type" prophecy is a physical thing or demonstrated action that is fulfilled in a spiritual context. The "type" is the shadow; the "anti-type" is its substance which has created the shadow. See this language used in Col. 2:16–17 and Heb. 10:1.)

God's Promise to David: David, the king of Israel, wanted to build a temple for God in Jerusalem, but God did not want a man of war and bloodshed to build a place of peaceful worship (1 Chron. 17:1–15, 28:2–3). Instead, God promised him an eternal kingdom with (by implication) a transcendent King (2 Sam. 7:12–16). While the historical ascension of this transcendent King is rooted in human lineage and OT prophecy (see Rom. 1:1–4, for example), God put the plan for this King into motion before the world was made (Eph. 3:11, Tim. 1:7–8).

God was not merely extending David's human kingdom into an ethereal and universal kingdom; He was bringing *His* kingdom into its new phase through His Son. David was a mere prototype; he was the shadow while Christ is the substance.

> When giving David assurance, God spoke of making David's kingdom permanent by placing on of his descendants on his throne… It makes no sense to have Christ on David's throne and the kingdom not be David's kingdom. Of course there are some differences! But it's crucial for us to see the continuity between the OT promises and the NT fulfillment.[19]

God's kingdom has always existed. Yet the means to bring *human beings* (made in God's image) into this kingdom has not always existed. The eternal plan to put Christ on the throne to rule over God's kingdom was necessary for this to happen.

Putting Christ on the throne included, however, all that led up to this: Christ had to leave heaven behind, come to earth as a man, live a perfect life, be killed on a cross, rise from the dead, and then ascend from earth into heaven. Once He had accomplished this, the kingdom of God could then be ready to receive the souls of people faithful to God. These souls include faithful men and women who have preceded Jesus' life in time as well as the faithful who came after Him.[20]

But we are getting ahead of ourselves. First, we need to appreciate the development of this kingdom throughout the Bible. Then we will see Jesus' kingdom teachings in a grander, fuller light than we may have seen previously.

The Tower of Babel: In Gen. 11:1–9, we see the entire human race, in essence, coming together to build a tower that would reach up to the sky. It was not only the height of this tower (known to us as the tower of Babel) that was significant, but what it communicated: men did not need God to make them important—they could do this alone. They did not need God to reach the heavens (so to speak)—they could reach it by their own wisdom, strength, and engineering. They did not need God to unify them—they could unify themselves by their own decrees, under their own terms, and according to their own definitions.

This is all evident in their own statement: "They said, 'Come, let us build for ourselves a city, and a tower whose top will reach into heaven, and let us make for ourselves a name, otherwise we will be scattered abroad over the face of the whole earth'" (Gen. 11:4).[21] This was in defiance of what God had told Adam, to "Be fruitful and multiply, and fill the earth" (Gen. 1:28).

What they did not realize, of course (among other things), was that a common language provided for their unified efforts. God easily frustrated their collective efforts by dividing this common language into a variety of languages, thus "confusing" the people and destroying their unity. As a result, all those who spoke a particular language banded together and left this man-made city, and "the LORD scattered them abroad over the face of the whole earth" (Gen. 11:9).

This event may seem like a weird, isolated incident that is as quickly forgotten (in the pages of the OT record) as it appeared. A worldwide campaign, a massive engineering enterprise (possibly years or decades in the making), and the unprecedented and spontaneous introduction of a diversity of languages are all summed up in nine verses. One wonders, upon initial observation, what the purpose of this account might be. In hindsight, there seems to be good reason for it. God did want humanity to have a singular language and a collective effort toward a common goal, but on His terms, not theirs. In Acts 2, Jews from all over the Roman Empire came together to observe Pentecost, but in doing so they heard God's revealed message—a message of truth that called them to a collective effort toward a collective goal. Truth is God's language; human faith is the collective effort; and the proclamation of the kingdom of God is its goal.

Immediately after the tower of Babel incident, God summoned a man named Abram from the far east and told him to leave his father's family and head toward Canaan (Gen. 12:1–3). (Terah, Abram's father, "served other gods" and Abram may have, too, until God called him; see Josh. 24:2–3.) While God did not use the word "kingdom" in His conversations with Abram, He implied it in the text. The mass of human beings that began the tower of Babel were building a kingdom for themselves—one that God quickly and permanently ended. Then God began unveiling His *own* kingdom plans—one that would not be dependent upon human power, one that would bless "all the families of the earth" (Gen. 12:3).

God Began to Unveil His Kingdom: Thus, as early as Gen. 12, we see God giving us glimpses into what He had planned for all eternity. Human power and human authority would not define His kingdom; His kingdom would transcend all the problems, corruptions, and limitations of any human king or kingdom. A new "David" would oversee His kingdom—One whose lineage came through King David's genealogy but incomprehensibly exceeded David and all his posterity. This new "David" would rule with heavenly wisdom, perfect ability, infallible justice, and amazing compassion. He would be introduced to humankind as a marvelous Child, indicating His newness, innocence, and faithfulness to His Father, as Isaiah proclaimed:

> For a child will be born to us, a son will be given to us; and the government will rest on His shoulders; and His name will be called Wonderful Counselor, Mighty God, Eternal Father, Prince of Peace. There will be no end to the increase of His government

or of peace, on the throne of David and over his kingdom, to establish it and to uphold it with justice and righteousness from then on and forevermore. The zeal of the LORD of hosts will accomplish this. (Isa. 9:6–7)

This Child would come through "the root of Jesse" and would rule over the people of Israel but also the entire world.[22]

> Then a shoot will spring from the stem of Jesse, and a branch from his roots will bear fruit. The Spirit of the LORD will rest on Him, the spirit of wisdom and understanding, the spirit of counsel and strength, the spirit of knowledge and the fear of the LORD. And He will delight in the fear of the LORD, and He will not judge by what His eyes see, nor make a decision by what His ears hear; but with righteousness He will judge the poor, and decide with fairness for the afflicted of the earth; and He will strike the earth with the rod of His mouth, and with the breath of His lips He will slay the wicked. Also righteousness will be the belt about His loins, and faithfulness the belt about His waist. (Isa. 11:1–5)

This transcendent Child-King would be innocent, righteous, and infallibly wise. He would be the greatest ruler the world has ever known. He would not be a passive, quiet, and uninvolved King; He would fiercely protect the weak and helpless—those who were weak and helpless through circumstances beyond their control—but He would also fight against His enemies. He would not be afraid to speak the truth or defend it as needed; He would not sit back and allow His people to be exploited, abused, and destroyed, but would rise to their defense and vindicate them in the end.

The Good Shepherd: As Israel sank deeper and deeper into apostasy and idolatry in the centuries following David's rule, the "shepherds of Israel"—kings, princes, priests, judges, and elders—made themselves wealthy, powerful, and fat at the expense of the common people (Ezek. 34:1–10, 18–21). They were awful shepherds: instead of tending their flock, they sucked all the life from it and then trampled it over as something unimportant and expendable. God was, not surprisingly, filled with wrath and indignation toward these shepherds. They had not only neglected their moral responsibility to the people, but they also defied God's law and showed no respect for God or His sheep.

God's response was to reveal (in prophecy) His own hand-picked Shepherd—a virtuous, morally perfect, and fully capable Man who would govern God's people without any hint of human frailty (Jer. 30:9, Ezek. 34:23–24, and 37:24–25). This promise was given to the nation of Israel (which included both the northern and southern tribes of Israel), which makes sense. Isaiah, Jeremiah, and Ezekiel were Israelite prophets who spoke to Israelites about covenant terms, national concerns, and future expectations all pertaining to Israel. The kingdom of God, under the benevolent rule of the prophetic coming "David," was to replace the human-led kingdom of Israel which human sin, human failure, and conflicts of interest had compromised.

This Shepherd/King would not occupy a physical throne in Jerusalem. God promised that no descendant of Coniah (a.k.a. Jeconiah, king of Judah) would ever sit on the throne of David or rule in Judah ever again (Jer. 22:24–30). This does not mean there could never be a descendant of David who would rule as the King of Israel; it only means that this King would not rule on this earth. His kingdom, while based upon David's throne and lineage, would be "not of this realm" (John 18:36).

Anticipation of Universal Salvation: While the Messiah ("David") fulfilled God's promises to provide Israel with a glorious King, and to invite all Israelites into a glorious kingdom, He did not limit His promise to Israel. Jesus identified Himself as the good Shepherd, which not only alludes to the *role* of a shepherd but also as a fulfillment of the *prophecies* concerning the Shepherd/David in *Ezekiel*. But He also looked beyond the nation of Israel: "I have other sheep, which are not of this fold; I must bring them also, and they will hear My voice; and they will become one flock with one shepherd" (John 10:16). Christ would not only be Israel's Shepherd but that of whoever heard His voice (John 10:27–28).

Thus, God's intention, through His Son's leadership, was to bring salvation to the entire world—to all nations, regardless of ethnicity. Paul speaks of this as a "mystery" that was once hidden from God's people but "has now been revealed to His holy apostles and prophets in the Spirit."[23] This universal offering of salvation has always been God's "eternal purpose which He carried out in Christ Jesus our Lord" (Eph. 3:1–11). In the messianic Servant Songs of *Isaiah*, God makes His intentions clear:

> [God] says [to the Messiah], "It is too small a thing that You should be My Servant to raise up the tribes of Jacob and to restore the preserved ones of Israel; I will also make You a light of the nations [i.e., Gentiles] so that My salvation may reach to the end of the earth." Thus says the LORD, the Redeemer of Israel and its Holy One, to the despised One, to the One abhorred by the nation, to the Servant of rulers, "Kings will see and arise, princes will also bow down, because of the LORD who is faithful, the Holy One of Israel who has chosen You." (Isa. 49:6–7, bracketed words are mine)

In Isa. 55:1–7, God invited "every one who thirsts" to "listen, that you may live" and to enter "an everlasting covenant…according to the faithful mercies shown to David" (compare Psalm 89:2–4). This invitation was intended for Israelites who had gone astray, but one cannot help but notice the universal application of this passage. God meant this invitation for the entire human race.

Through Christ's mediation (His virtuous life, sacrificial death, and taking His seat at the right hand of God), God's gospel would invite all people into fellowship with Him. Thus, Christ did not die only for Israelites, or only for Christians; rather, "He Himself is the propitiation for our sins; and not for ours only, but also for those of the whole world" (1 John 2:2).[24]

Even in Isaiah's day, a Gentile (non-Jew) could enter a covenant with God through his allegiance to the Law of Moses, but the prophet's passage goes far beyond this. This universal salvation—where "universal" refers to its availability, not its application—could not have been fully realized until God's kingdom had been given to the Savior of the entire world. God's "eternal purpose" required a sequence of events in both human history and divine protocol. The King of Israel is also Israel's Messiah (which means "God's Anointed One"), who is also the Redeemer of humankind. This Messiah must:

- come into the world (Isa. 9:6, "a Child will be given to us…").
- prove His virtue and ability to lead through His love, compassion, and righteousness (Isa. 42:1–4, He will be God's "chosen one in whom My soul delights").
- die as a sin offering for His people (Isa. 53:1–12).
- rise from the dead (as implied in Psalm 16:8–11, 110:1, 89:2–4, 132:11, etc.).
- rise from this world to return to heaven (John 17:4–5, Acts 1:9–11).
- take His seat at the right hand of God, at which point His Father gives Him reign over His (God's) kingdom (Dan. 7:9–10, 13–14, Acts 2:33, Heb. 8:1, etc.).
- exercise His authority over both the visible and invisible worlds (Psalm 2:6–8, Eph. 1:19–21, Heb. 1:3–12, etc.).
- build His church, the sanctuary of all souls—past, present, and future—redeemed by His blood (Mat. 16:18, Eph. 1:22–23, Col. 1:18, etc.).

These things had to happen in this order. No part of this plan could be omitted or circumvented. God put this plan—a divine, eternal, and unstoppable plan—into motion from the beginning of the world. Christ was not simply a significant part of this plan; He *was the plan*. As Paul said:

> He made known to us the mystery of His will, according to His kind intention which He purposed in Him with a view to an administration suitable to the fullness of the times, that is, the summing up of all things in Christ, things in the heavens and things on the earth. (Eph. 1:9–10)

God unfolded this "mystery of His will" slowly but methodically over the centuries before Jesus came into the world. He began with Abram, making a promise to him in which "all the families of the earth will be blessed" (Gen. 12:3). The "mystery" was not only about salvation but also Jesus Christ's reign as King over God's kingdom: the one (salvation) was fully dependent upon the other (His reign as King).

The ancients were familiar with human kings and the great power they possessed over their respective kingdoms. In some cases, as with Nebuchadnezzar, the sovereign king of Babylon, those kings ruled over much of the known earth. However, no one ever predicted a King whose rule would be over *all* the earth *and* the unseen world as well. No one ever realized that this King would begin as a human Child upon the earth and ultimately take His seat at the right hand of God in heaven.

> Because God has revealed Himself in history, He has shown Himself to be the Lord of history. History is the scene of the divine activity. History, therefore, has a direction and a goal—the kingdom of God. The certainty of the future kingdom springs from faith in God's work of salvation in the history of Israel. This is the source of Israel's eschatology [i.e., study of the end times]. … The OT hope is always expressed in terms of Israel's future. Israel has been called to be God's people; God acts in history both to judge and bless His people; and God will finally bring His people into the salvation of His kingdom.[25]

In one of the earliest sermons preached concerning the gospel of Christ, Peter said to the Jews: "It is you who are the sons of the prophets and of the covenant which God made with your fathers, saying to Abraham, 'And in your seed all the families of the earth shall be blessed'" (Acts 3:25). God accomplished all this through the nation of Israel.

> [T]his rule of heaven and Kingship of Jehovah was the very substance of the Old Testament; the object of the calling and mission of Israel; the meaning of all its ordinances, whether civil or religious; the underlying idea of all its institutions. It

explained alike the history of the people, the dealings of God with them, and the prospects opened up by the prophets. Without it the Old Testament could not be understood; it gave perpetuity to its teaching, and dignity to its representations. This constituted alike the real contrast between Israel and the nations of antiquity, and Israel's real title to distinction. Thus the whole Old Testament was the preparatory presentation of the rule of heaven and of the Kingship of its Lord.[26]

God had fulfilled the transcendent plan which He had first disclosed to Abram two thousand years before Jesus entered the world. Christ is now the King, He has built His church, and He welcomes into it all who call upon the Lord for salvation.

Summary Thoughts: While His kingdom has always existed, God has not always explained it to the human world. There were good reasons for this, some of which we know and many which we will never know in this life. One reason was that the world simply was not yet ready to receive God's kingdom as He intended. Another was that His only begotten Son, Jesus, had to come into the world in the fullness of time ("at the right time"—Rom. 5:6). God never does things without purpose, a schedule, and optimum effectiveness.

Many kings of various moral dispositions oversaw the nation of Israel from David to Judah's exile into Babylonia (ca. 1000 to 586 BC). Over centuries, the nation suffered under the abuses, exploitations, and neglect of many of these kings as well as princes, priests, and elders. What the nation—and the world—needed was a transcendent King/Shepherd whose character and moral fitness would never be compromised by human sin or frailty. God slowly unveiled this model King and the nature of His rule through His prophets, and Isaiah in particular.

God's attention was not only on providing a glorious King for Israel but One that would rule over all Creation. He would not only provide a Redeemer for Israel but all humankind. This is what He had planned from the beginning. Its gradual prophetic emergence was because God was allowing all the right sequences of events and proper conditions to be fulfilled for bringing His Messiah into the world.

Redemption of human souls is the key to understanding God's kingdom and the King to whom He would entrust this kingdom. We will cover this subject in more detail shortly.

Chapter Three

The Nature of the Kingdom

The kingdom of God oversees all Creation, or all things that "have come into being" (John 1:3). God the Father, God the Son, and God the Spirit are divine Beings that have always existed. They are uncreated; there was never a time when they did not exist. Everything else, however, has a beginning point at which it began; prior to this, it did not exist. It is this—*all* of this, which includes all material, non-material, and living things—over which the kingdom of God reigns. This means that Christ, as King, reigns over all these things.

We are speaking of the kingdom of God here in its full description. God is "a great King" (Mal. 1:14) and His kingdom encompasses all that has come into being. He has given all authority to His Son to reign over this kingdom. This speaks of the kingdom in practical and legal terms. The kingdom of God is not Christ's church—an erroneous conclusion that has led people to misunderstand both the kingdom *and* the church. The kingdom, practically speaking, extends far beyond the church. (We will cover this in more detail in a later chapter.)

Kingdom of God/of Heaven: First, we need clarification on the two different phrases for what Jesus preached: "kingdom of God" and "kingdom of heaven." Matthew, in his gospel account, uses "of heaven" far more than "of God." "Heaven" in the Greek language referred to "the region above the sidereal [i.e., relating to the stars] heavens, the seat of an order of things eternal and consummately perfect, where God dwells and the other heavenly beings."[27] This is a suitable definition, as it defines the place of origin of this kingdom: it is not of this earth, not of this world (universe), and not of the physical realm.

> It is a kingdom of heaven because its origin, its end, its king, the character and destiny of its subjects, its laws, institutions, and privileges—all are heavenly. In the teaching of Christ and in

the apostolic writings the kingdom of the Messiah is the actual consummation of the prophetic idea of the rule of God, without any national limitation, so that participation therein rests only on faith in Jesus Christ, and on the moral renewal which is conditioned by the same.[28]

The "kingdom of heaven" is the reign of God *over* all Creation; "kingdom of God" is the manifestation of this heavenly reign *to* Creation. Yet, "the simple fact is that they are quite interchangeable."[29]

> In its broadest connotation the terms *"the kingdom of heaven,"* "the kingdom of God," or simply "the kingdom" (when the context makes clear that what is meant is "the kingdom of heaven or of God") *indicate God's kingship, rule or sovereignty*, recognized in the hearts and operative in the lives of His people, and effecting their *complete salvation*, their constitution as a *church*, and finally a redeemed *universe*."[30]

Whatever is "of heaven" is also "from above," where God is (see James' use of this in James 3:15, 17). Thus, whatever is of heaven is also of God; as God is "above" (being transcendent in nature and divine in origin), so is His kingdom. "For 'heaven' here is, according to a very current Jewish expression, a metonymy for God. It is the kingdom, which is governed not by earthly powers, but by heaven."[31]

A Spiritual Kingdom: We know that the kingdom of God is not a physical or geographical place. It is not something you can find on a map or visit in person. As God is spiritual in nature (John 4:24), so His kingdom is spiritual in nature. This does not mean that it does not really exist: "spiritual" does not mean pretend or conceptual but defines what is invisible to human sight. We can see the effects of the wind, but not the wind. We can see the effects of God's Spirit on those who are "born again," but He remains invisible (John 3:6–8). We can see the effects of (and we participate in the domain of) the kingdom of God, but we cannot see the King or His kingdom.

While the kingdom of God is spiritual in nature, its effects are not limited to the spiritual realm. For example, "No one has seen God at any time; if we love one another, God abides in us, and His love is perfected in us" (1 John 4:12). No one sees God, but He can be seen in His people. Likewise, no one can see God's kingdom, but His kingdom's influence can be seen in those who have become its citizens.

The kingdom can also be seen in its historical influence: the supremacy of Christ's reign would be "seen" through the destruction of Jerusalem and nation of Israel. This would happen in the lifetimes of those who were with the Lord in His ministry: "Truly I say to you, there are some of those who are standing here who will not taste death until they see the kingdom of God after it has come with power" (Mark 9:1; compare Luke 9:27).

While the kingdom is not all about "eating and drinking" (Rom. 14:27), it does directly affect those who do eat and drink—i.e., it permeates well beyond the mere practice of religion and into the physical and visible lives of its servants.

> Jesus assures Pilate in John 18:36 that His "kingdom is not of this world." Christ didn't wade into His throne through blood, smoke, fire, and treachery. It wasn't built on physical territory, He still is Lord of actual nations! His kingdom is "spiritual," but that doesn't mean it is confined to the inner world of personal religion or the invisible world of spirits.[32]

The effects of Christ's kingship are not limited to churches, church buildings, worship services, or even Christians' homes. The effects of Christ's work in His kingdom—whatever He accomplishes through the agency of the Holy Spirit—is not limited to these things, either. When we equate Christ's kingdom with His church (again, a wrong conclusion), we begin reducing the power of Christ's kingdom to the finite and human limitations of congregations of people.

Whatever is happening in the spiritual realm has a direct effect on our material, three-dimensional, and visible world. The book of *Revelation* confirms this. Things here are not always what they seem; what we see does not always accurately depict what is really happening behind the scenes. Dynamics within the spiritual world affect people and circumstances in the physical world. Christians are engaged in a spiritual battle (Eph. 6:12) yet we do not see or always experience the effects of that battle. Likewise, God abides in us, and we abide in Him (1 John 3:24), but we do not see or feel His presence.

God's kingdom is "not of this world" (John 18:36). This does not mean that it has no effect on this world but that it transcends this world in every respect. The kingdom's work, influence, and contention with evil affect those who are working *in* it as well as those who are working *against* it. Someone has said, "God is always up to something," which means that He is always active to fulfill His will, always vigilant for His people, and never disconnected from His Creation.

As King, Christ shares these functions and is Himself always working behind the scenes toward a known and purposeful end. As we have discussed, the purpose of Christ's kingship over God's kingdom has everything to do with the redemption of human souls. The Father, Son, and Spirit are actively engaged in this purpose.

Thus, the kingdom of God is:

- spiritual in nature and otherworldly in design. It operates in the spiritual realm, yet its effects are everywhere in the realm of humankind.
- eternal in nature (2 Peter 1:11). It is not a stop-gap measure, incidental work, or temporary phase. As God's reign is eternal, so His kingdom will endure forever. Those who align themselves with God's kingdom on earth (through their allegiance to Christ the King) will reign with Him in the eternity to come.
- immune to human change, influence, or customization. No person can alter or amend God's kingdom any more than he can change God Himself. People do not influence the kingdom; it is the kingdom that, if anything, influences people.

> ❏ not dependent upon who does or does not believe in it. Satan derives his power from sinners; it is dependent upon people giving him control over them. God, however, is self-existing and self-sustaining. God's absolute and unlimited authority is the power behind His kingdom; He does not need or rely upon human approval. People can say or believe whatever they want about God's kingdom (as they also do regarding God, Christ, the hereafter, etc.) but it remains what it is—unchanged, uncorrupted, and undeterred from its goals.

This means that God is in control of His Creation, and all this control is now exercised through the royal reign of His Son, Jesus Christ. It does not matter how we perceive that control in the natural world because, given the scope of God's knowledge, power, and eternal nature, there is far more that we do not understand than what we do understand.

> Because we live in a world of "natural law" and in social intercourse with beings who make free decisions, it shouldn't surprise us that "senseless" things occur in life or that cruel things are perpetuated by people against people. It yet remains that God is in control of history and is working toward the completion of His grand purpose in Christ. Believers may debate how rigid that control is but they all maintain that God is in complete control and that His purpose will be accomplished."[33]

A Multi-dimensional Kingdom: Some view the kingdom of God as "multidimensional." This simply means that there are various aspects of it, diverse ways to explain it, and different ways of understanding it. For example, when Jesus said, "the kingdom of God is at hand" (Mark 1:15), He was speaking of a particular phase of the kingdom, not its full and timeless existence. God's kingdom has always been; it is not "at hand" in the sense that it is about to begin, but something *about* or *within* the kingdom *is* "at hand."

It is not good Bible study to limit one's understanding of a subject to only one dimension when in fact the subject is multifaceted. For example, limiting the subject of God's love to "He cares about us" fails to consider what He has done because of His love, all that His love does for us now, and what He will allow to happen to us even though He cares about us. We cannot cram God's love into a single, personal, and preferential aspect when in fact it has many aspects.

This is also true regarding the kingdom of God. We may define the kingdom with a simple overarching conclusion (e.g., God's rule over all Creation) but there are myriads of facets to this. "It won't do to proclaim only the inner kingdom of religious experience, the ecclesiastical kingdom of church expansion, the social kingdom of a transformed society, the eschatological kingdom of the apocalyptists, or the transported and transformed kingdom under the name 'heaven.' Making one truth the only truth is to be avoided in any sphere of knowledge."[34] There is no singular truth about the kingdom; indeed, it has many truths, none of which contradict each other or conflict with God's own holy nature.

It is for this reason that Jesus described the kingdom of God (or, of heaven) variously. There is no single "way" to see or describe it. As a diamond is a single gem with many facets, so the kingdom of God is a single concept (God's rule over all Creation) with many facets, operations, applications, and effects. Think about these facets in Jesus' description of the kingdom:

- **a man sowing seed in a field** (Mat. 13:24): the kingdom work is active in the unconverted world, despite unbelievers, false converts, and backsliders. The same message of the kingdom falls upon different hearts, producing different results. Yet, despite even negative results, God is accomplishing His kingdom work in all those who hear of it. A decision to reject the kingdom is equal to a decision to submit to it: in both cases, the "seed" forced a conviction from each heart upon whom it was sown.
- **a mustard seed which grows into a large tree** (Mat. 13:31, Mark 4:30–32): from a human perspective, the kingdom appears to "grow" as we become more aware of it. In reality, it is already fully mature, completely developed, and lacking in nothing. Its alleged

increase refers to its having exceeded all original expectations, just as a large tree grows from a minuscule seed that you can put on your fingertip.
- **leaven which permeated an entire lump of dough** (Mat. 13:33): the work of the kingdom is persistent, as well as consistent (think of Isa. 55:8–11).
- **a treasure found in a field** (Mat. 13:44): to "find" the kingdom is to realize that it exists and that what it offers the sinner is priceless and worth the loss of everything else.
- **a pearl of great price** (Mat. 13:45): while similar to the "treasure" application, this is a different perspective. In this case, there are many pearls (many kingdoms) in the world but there is only one that is worth a believer's entire investment.
- **a dragnet pulling in all sorts of fish** (Mat. 13:47): God invites all people to enter the kingdom (a phrase which we will expound upon later). While many may respond in one form or another, only faithful followers are fit for service in His kingdom work.
- **a king settling accounts with his slaves** (Mat. 18:23): forgiveness is obtained through the King's mercy and grace, but this requires that forgiven people also be forgiving (Mat. 6:14–15).
- **a landowner hiring slaves throughout the day to work in his vineyard** (Mat. 20:1): all who work in God's kingdom receive the same reward—salvation and a spiritual inheritance—and all who become its citizens have agreed to this. Level of ability, level of responsibility, and the amount of time served has no bearing upon this, only each person's faithfulness to the Master.
- **a wedding feast a king gives for his son** (Mat. 22:2): being invited into the kingdom requires something of those who "attend." This is not a come-as-you-are event, but one for which each person must be gratefully prepared.
- **ten virgins who await the bride and bridegroom** (Mat. 25:1): while everyone in the kingdom has the same opportunity, not all equally prepare themselves for what God expects of its citizens or for what is coming.
- **the emergence of a fruit-bearing plant apart from human intervention** (Mark 4:26–29): while believers actively participate in the work of God's kingdom, He does things that we cannot do, see,

or even fully understand. We cannot think that the success of His kingdom rests upon our shoulders.

Which of these parables fully describes the kingdom of God? None of them. Yet all of them give us another sense or understanding of this kingdom. Jesus never said, "This is exactly what the kingdom is." And He never said, "This is entirely how the kingdom is described." He used parables, metaphors, and comparative illustrations to depict one aspect or another of the kingdom. No one of these are a complete picture; in fact, the sum of them still does not fully describe all that the King and His kingdom is or does.

The only information we have about God is what He has chosen to reveal to us. We cannot know anything about Him or the spiritual realm that He has not revealed, since He is a spiritual being, and we only know the visible and material world. So it is with His kingdom: we only know what He has disclosed to us through His Son, apostles, and written word. When Jesus unveiled various aspects of the kingdom through His parables and illustrations, He only told us what He wanted us to know, that which was relevant to our understanding of it. Remember what Moses told Israel: "The secret things belong to the LORD our God, but the things revealed belong to us and to our sons forever, that we may observe all the words of this law" (Deut. 29:29). This applies to us in principle as well.

The presentation of the Kingdom through parables "must now be for decision."[35] In other words, Jesus' use of parables was not merely for instruction, mere improvement of understanding, or colorful entertainment. Hearing these was not meant to be a mere academic exercise in the study of difficult things. Rather, in hearing the parables, one would receive the message of the kingdom, another would reject it; in both cases, a decision was required, and a decision was made—not by God but by each respective hearer.[36]

Jesus admitted to His disciples that not everyone was going to grasp His parables concerning the kingdom of God—at least, not right away—but that this was the means He chose to disclose it (Mat. 13:10–17). The "mysteries of the kingdom of heaven" were not intended to be known up front. Even Jesus' own disciples did not understand them all (Mat. 13:36, for example). "Jesus' speaking in parables has a two-fold effect: on the one hand it is a revelation, on the other it veils something."[37] In time, the preaching of Jesus' gospel would reveal all the "mysteries" He intended for us to know (Eph. 3:1–7).

Summary Thoughts: God's kingdom rules over all that He has created. This is a statement of fact; there is no disputing this; it is not a question that needs answered. But God's rule over Creation is not the only way to view His kingdom, His rule, or His work. Jesus' diversity of similes and explanations concerning the kingdom clues us into the diversity of the kingdom itself. It is not a simple concept; therefore, a simple explanation will not do it justice.

God's kingdom is spiritual in nature and therefore is out of reach of human tinkering or corruption. He allows us to "see" His kingdom through faith, and we do see its effects in the form of changed hearts and lives. But He does not allow us to interfere with it through making changes, amendments, or creative interpretations. Regardless of our grasp of the kingdom, or even our rejection of it, it remains what God forever intended it to be.

Jesus never came out and said, "This is what the kingdom is all about." Like so much of Scripture, God wants us to be students of His word rather than mere readers of it. Reading about the kingdom takes us only so far; studying about it takes us much further. Even so, we can only know what God has revealed and no more. We can postulate, speculate, and even debate beyond this, but we cannot factually ascertain anything more than what God has declared. And He has not declared anything to me differently than what He has declared to you and to all humankind.

Chapter Four

The Sons of the Kingdom

Those who identify as Christians today tend also to identify as citizens of God's kingdom. There is nothing wrong with this dual identification, since whoever belongs to Christ (in His "body," the church) also is a citizen of God's kingdom (i.e., he subjects himself to the King's authority).

This does not make the two things (the kingdom and the church) the same thing but only that legitimate participation in one necessitates such participation in the other. Yet before we begin talking about the church, we need to talk about the kingdom since this preceded the church, both historically and sequentially. No one could have become a member of Christ's church unless or until God had put His kingdom under Christ's authority.

God offered the Israelites the original public disclosure of and introduction into the kingdom. Ideally, they were supposed to be "sons of the kingdom" (Mat. 13:38), the initial heirs of God's long-awaited regeneration of Israel under the rule of His Messiah (Christ). It is important to see the predominate focus of Jesus' preaching on this point. Otherwise, every time we read "the kingdom" in the gospel accounts, we tend to think He was talking only to Christians (or about the church) when in fact He was most often speaking to the Jews about what God had long promised them.

The Old Testament Promises: While there are obscured references to the coming Messiah in the Law of Moses (see Gen. 49:10 and Deut. 18:18, for example), the first real glimpse we get of this is in God's promise to David, king of Israel. David wanted to build a temple for God in Jerusalem (since the original Mosaic tabernacle had been destroyed, and there was not a proper place for the ark of the covenant—2 Sam.

7:1–2), but God refused this because David was a man of war and bloodshed. Instead, it would be his son Solomon who would build God's house in Jerusalem (2 Sam. 7:12–13, 1 Kings 5:3–4).

But God promised David something far better than the honor of building a physical temple. He promised him an eternal kingdom, with one of his own descendants sitting as its eternal king (2 Sam. 7:16). The psalmists and prophets likewise underscored this:

- "The LORD has sworn to David a truth from which He will not turn back: 'Of the fruit of your body I will set upon your throne'" (Psalm 132:11).
- "There will be no end to the increase of His [Messiah's] government or of peace, on the throne of David and over his kingdom, to establish it and to uphold it with justice and righteousness from then on and forevermore" (Isa. 9:7).
- "And I, the LORD, will be their God, and My servant David will be prince among them; I the LORD have spoken" (Ezek. 34:24).
- "My servant David will be king over them, and they will all have one shepherd; and they will walk in My ordinances and keep My statutes and observe them. They will live on the land that I gave to Jacob My servant, in which your fathers lived; and they will live on it, they, and their sons and their sons' sons, forever; and David My servant will be their prince forever" (Ezek. 37:24–25).

The word "Messiah" means "anointed one," and occurs only once in the OT with reference to the coming king of Israel (Dan. 9:25). But the prophetic "David" is used several times, as well as "Branch" (Isa. 11:1, Jer. 23:5, 33:15, etc.), a reference to the regeneration of Israel from the dead, "like a root out of parched ground" (Isa. 53:2). In fact, "David" became the prophetic code word for the Jews' coming Messiah.

While the northern tribes of Israel disappeared into Assyrian captivity and the southern tribes languished for seventy years in Babylonian captivity (and most captive Jews remained there), the Jews longed for national redemption and the restoration of their once unified kingdom.

This new David would usher in this restoration, a time of great glory and prosperity, as indicated in Isa. 60. We will consider an excerpt here, addressed to Israel:

> Arise, shine; for your light has come, and the glory of the Lord has risen upon you. For behold, darkness will cover the earth and deep darkness the peoples; but the Lord will rise upon you and His glory will appear upon you. Nations will come to your light, and kings to the brightness of your rising. (Isa. 60:1–3)

The Jews who returned from Babylonian captivity to Judea (beginning ca. 536 BC) longed for this glorious restoration of Israel. They assumed that their coming King would reign upon a throne in Jerusalem, casting off the oppression of secular governments and heathen rulers that plagued the Jews throughout the intertestamental period (ca. 450 BC–AD 30).

The Jews also assumed that this reign would be political, national, and geographical. It would be political because their King would oversee the people according to His own authority and exercise of justice. It would be national because it would make the Israelite nation the center of the world (for a thousand years, they believed) and all the other nations would be subject to it. It would be geographical because this center of the world was in the original territory given to Israel, as apportioned by Joshua, and the city of Jerusalem would be its capital. "In the Old Testament perspective, the coming of God's Kingdom is viewed as a single great event: a mighty manifestation of God's power which would sweep away the wicked kingdoms of human sovereignty and would fill all the earth with righteousness."[38]

Such were beliefs the Jews held in anticipation of their Messiah. By the time Jesus came into the world, the Jewish nation had not heard from God's prophets for over four hundred years. The last thing they heard was that "Elijah" would come to announce the presentation of God's Messiah: "Behold, I am going to send you Elijah the prophet before the coming of the great and terrible day of the Lord. He will restore the hearts of the fathers to their children and the hearts of the children to their fathers" (Mal. 4:5–6). This "Elijah" was John the Baptist (Luke 1:13–17), as Jesus confirmed (Mat. 11:14).

John the Baptist did not preach to the world or evangelize among the Gentiles; his ministry was only to the Jews. Some listened to John and were baptized by him (as a sign of their repentance and renewal of their covenant to God; see Luke 3:3–5). Others rejected John's baptism as being from heaven, thus resisting his message of preparation for the coming King (Luke 7:24–30).

Jesus, as He came into the world, was not identified as the king over all Creation but as the King of Israel (Luke 1:31–33, John 1:49, etc.) or the King of the Jews (Mat. 2:2). Jesus referred to Himself in third person as a divine King (Mat. 25:34) but admitted openly that He was indeed the King of the Jews (Luke 23:3). People referred to Him as "son of David" multiple times in the gospel accounts. The Jewish leaders knew that the Messiah had to be of David's physical lineage (Mat. 22:42) to fulfill God's promise to David for an eternal kingdom.[39]

Jesus was the "Son" (descendant) of David, but He was also the "David," the "Branch" of OT messianic prophecy. The physical connection to King David provided a royal lineage and thus the right to rule over Israel. His spiritual sonship to God provided a far transcendent royal lineage and thus the right to rule over all of Creation. Paul linked these two roles in his opening to *Romans*:

> Paul, a bond-servant of Christ Jesus, called as an apostle, set apart for the gospel of God, which He promised beforehand through His prophets in the holy Scriptures, concerning His Son, who was born of a descendant of David according to the flesh, who was declared the Son of God with power by the resurrection from the dead… (Rom. 1:1–4)

Jesus told Pontius Pilate, the Roman governor who would hand Him over to be crucified, that "For this [i.e., to be King of the Jews] I have been born, and for this I have come into the world" (John 18:37). And, since no king is of any use without a people and/or dominion over which to reign, Jesus also told Pilate that He had a kingdom (John 18:36).

So then, Jesus was born to reign as King, and He would most certainly oversee a kingdom. However, His kingdom is not of this world. This means His entire ministry, while performed on earth in midst of multitudes of human witnesses, remained otherworldly in its purpose and fulfillment. He was not seeking a political kingship; His throne was in heaven, not in Jerusalem (or anywhere else on earth). He was not seeking to re-establish the Israelite nation as a separate people with exclusive covenantal privileges that set them above the rest of the world. He was not seeking to limit His kingdom to the physical boundaries of the ancient nation of Israel. Consider this exchange between Jesus and the Samaritan woman at Jacob's well:

> "Our fathers worshiped in this mountain, and you people say that in Jerusalem is the place where men ought to worship." Jesus said to her, "Woman, believe Me, an hour is coming when neither in this mountain [i.e., Mt Gerizim in Samaria] nor in Jerusalem will you worship the Father. You [Samaritans] worship what you do not know; we [Jews] worship what we know, for salvation is from the Jews. But an hour is coming, and now is, when the true worshipers will worship the Father in spirit and truth; for such people the Father seeks to be His worshipers. (John 4:20–24, bracketed words are mine)

The Jews of Jesus' day accurately saw themselves as the recipients of God's OT promises. They equated this to the coming of God's kingdom among them and regarded themselves as the primary beneficiaries of its glory. They were familiar enough with the messages of the prophets to have a basic understanding of this kingdom and its implications. However, three things they often did not see correctly:

- **First**, entrance into the kingdom of God was not to be based upon ethnicity, heritage, or national distinction, but upon faith in, surrender to, and allegiance toward the King (Christ). Those Jews who refused to honor the King would forfeit entrance into His kingdom; those who refused to change their hearts to accommodate kingdom teaching (consider Luke 5:36–39 here) would also forfeit their opportunity. Jesus' message to the Jews was not merely "The kingdom of God is upon you," but "Get your hearts ready to *participate* in this kingdom." The entire premise of Jesus' sermon on the mount, for example, was "Get your heart right for God's kingdom" (Mat. 5–7).
- **Second**, God (and Christ) intended for a universal gospel—one available to any person—rather than a Jewish gospel, or a mere reboot of Judaism.[40] While the Jews would be the first to receive the invitation to hear this gospel and enter Christ's kingdom, they would not be the only ones (John 10:16). And all those who obeyed the gospel would be on par with all others who did the same thing, without any reference to earthly status (Gal. 3:26–29). As all people would come to God as sinners, they would be saved as saints; "For there is no partiality with God" (Rom. 2:11).
- **Third**, the Jews did not understand the earthly ministry, or even the divine nature, of their coming King. To them, the Messiah was to be a glorified man, endued with supernatural power and unflinching courage, but they did not anticipate a divine Being coming to them in the form of a human being. Their Messiah was a great warrior, a heavenly statesman, powerful, invincible, victorious, immortal. They also did not anticipate that this Messiah would have to suffer incomprehensible pain, humiliation, and death. The idea of a suffering Savior was unthinkable to them.[41] Personal suffering implied wrongdoing (see John 9:1–2, for example) or some kind of moral defect; only criminals and wicked people suffered punishment.[42] A man nailed to a cross was a man not worthy to identify with God, not worthy to live, and certainly not worthy to be their Messiah. Thus, Jesus' crucifixion became a "stumbling block"—a tripping point, or a catalyst for unbelief—to the Jews (1 Cor. 1:22–23).

These three mindsets blinded many Jews to whom it was that was teaching them, walking through their cities, and performing numerous signs. The evidence was right in front of them, yet they could not see it because their hearts were closed and Jesus, despite the wonderful things He did, did not meet their messianic expectations. Some questioned this, of course, by citing the most obvious and stubborn evidence: the miracles that Jesus produced.

- "Rabbi, we [Pharisees who secretly believe] know that You have come from God as a teacher; for no one can do these signs that You do unless God is with him" (John 3:2, bracketed words are mine).
- "But many of the crowd believed in Him; and they were saying, 'When the Christ comes, He will not perform more signs than those which this man has, will He?'" (John 7:31).
- "Therefore some of the Pharisees were saying, 'This man is not from God, because He does not keep the Sabbath.' But others were saying, 'How can a man who is a sinner perform such signs?' And there was a division among them" (John 9:16).
- "Since the beginning of time it has never been heard that anyone opened the eyes of a person born blind. If this man were not from God, He could do nothing" (John 9:32–33).

The Leaders' Influence: The Jewish leadership remained unconvinced, however. They did not want to give up their privileged status, control of the people, and economic wealth that came with status and control (Luke 16:14). They admitted privately that Jesus was performing miracles (John 11:47) yet refused to accept the implications of this. In their eyes, they had much to lose if they surrendered to this Man; they even went against their own conscience to maintain a party line that publicly rejected Jesus' claims.

This is most evident in John 12:42–43: "many even of the rulers believed in Him, but because of the Pharisees they were not confessing Him, for fear that they would be put out of the synagogue; for they loved the approval of men rather than the approval of God." This craving for human approval was like a powerful drug; their irrational response to

Jesus' teachings and miracles is proof of a satanic influence over their hearts. Later, Paul would say that they were blinded to the truth, "for if they had understood it they would not have crucified the Lord of glory" (1 Cor. 2:8). Later, too, as the gospel of Christ was spreading, "a great many of the priests were becoming obedient to the faith" (Acts 6:7). But these things came later, after they had carried out the deed of crucifying their own Messiah.

Some Jews assumed that if Jesus were the Messiah, the Jewish leadership would have agreed with Him and given Him their endorsement. Since the leadership did not approve of Him, the people reasoned that Jesus must be just another fraud or opportunist. They could not deny the authenticity of His miracles, but this was not enough to overcome their hardness of heart.

Miracles never saved anyone; people can reject miracles as easily as they can the truth when their heart is already predisposed to unbelief. As Abraham said in Jesus' account of the rich man and Lazarus, "If they do not listen to Moses and the Prophets, they will not be persuaded even if someone rises from the dead" (Luke 16:31). It was, after all, Moses and the prophets that spoke of the coming Messiah (John 5:46–47).

Kingdom Fervor: Even so, Jesus most certainly excited the Jews' messianic hope. This is why many came to listen to Him, watched Him perform signs, and even followed Him around the countryside. Expectations ran high, even fever-pitched at times. The Jews were anxious for a national hero to liberate them from Rome's oversight, abuses, and taxes. They viewed Jesus with starry-eyed optimism that He would be this great Liberator and even wanted to expedite His plans by making Him their king by force (John 6:15).

> In making the kingdom or kingship of God the theme of His preaching, Jesus did not have to arouse interest in His message or to explain to the people what He meant. Although their ideas were often misguided, especially as a result of their narrowly nationalistic hopes, the people had some idea of what the

kingship of God meant. At first sight, therefore, the new element in the teaching of Jesus was concerned not with the character of the kingdom but with the time of its coming.[43]

Some Jews believed that the kingdom of God "was going to appear immediately" with a sudden and miraculous transition (Luke 19:11). In response to this, Jesus told a sobering parable that those citizens who rejected their King—the One who was speaking to them in the moment—would be destroyed (Luke 19:12–27). Despite this, when Jesus rode into Jerusalem on a donkey colt a week before His crucifixion, the people proclaimed, "Blessed is the coming kingdom of our father David" (Mark 11:10). The fact that Jesus was riding on a donkey and not a white stallion was lost on them, as was the spiritual nature of His kingdom.[44]

Even Jesus' disciples had grandiose ideas about Jesus and His kingdom. The mother of James and John requested of Jesus that her sons would sit on either side of Him "in Your kingdom." Yet Jesus told these two men, "You do not know what you are asking" (Mat. 20:20–23). This was true: they did not understand the nature of their Master's kingdom; they were blind to what He would have to undergo on His way to receiving that kingdom (see Mat. 16:21–23 and Luke 9:45).

Jesus went on to say, "My cup you shall drink; but to sit on My right and on My left, this is not Mine to give, but it is for those for whom it has been prepared by My Father," which indicates once again that Jesus was not creating a new kingdom (or a kingdom of His own) but was inheriting a kingdom from His Father.

On another occasion, someone invited Jesus to a meal in his home. Jesus pointed out the fact that the other guests were seeking the best seats at the table (Luke 14:7–14). He followed this observation with a parable that taught humility and deference. On the heels of this, however, someone announced, "Blessed is everyone who will eat bread in the kingdom of God!" (Luke 14:15). The idea here was that when the King/Messiah came to power, He would provide an abundance of food and drink, that the nation of Israel would once again enjoy a time of immense prosperity (as in the days of King Solomon). This man also assumed, judging from Jesus' response to him, that he himself would be in this kingdom simply because he was a Jew.

Jesus answered this man with another parable about those whom God (the "man") invited into His kingdom but who did not value that invitation (Luke 14:24). These people did not come to the feast prepared for them, and "they all alike began to make excuses" for their absences. In so doing, they dishonored not only the priceless privilege the host had offered them (a seat at his grand feast) but they dishonored the host himself (who shouldered the entire cost of this feast).

This parable is unmistakably a condemnation against careless, assumptive, and proud Jews who felt entitled to the kingdom simply because they were God's people by covenant. Not only does Jesus say (through the parable) that such men would not be in the kingdom, but that the kingdom invitation would go to those who were *not* Jews, even men who seemed unworthy to attend such a privileged feast.

Sons of the Kingdom: The Jews were the "sons of the kingdom" but many did not respect their sonship or the covenantal obligations they had to their Father. They claimed God as their spiritual Father and Abraham as their ancestral father (John 8:33, 41). They wanted the privilege of sonship without the moral responsibility of what this required of them. Based on future experiences, some saw this new "kingdom life" as merely a modified extension of Judaism. In this view, they (the Jews) would still maintain their privileged status as a favored people even if God did allow Gentiles to participate in it. In other words, they saw themselves always as first-class citizens of the kingdom and all others as second-class citizens.

Interestingly, the phrase "sons of the kingdom" is used only twice in Scripture—once negatively, once positively. In the negative usage (Mat. 8:11–12), the "sons" were meant to be the heirs of the Messiah's kingdom but forfeited this because of their lack of *faith* in the Messiah. They did not believe Him, even when He walked their streets, spoke to their faces, and performed many miracles to prove that both He and His message were of God (John 10:37–38).

In contrast, a Gentile centurion[45] displayed such great faith in Jesus that he knew that if He would just "say the word," He could heal his sick servant (Mat. 8:5–10). In response to this, Jesus talked about the "sons of the kingdom" being "cast out into the outer darkness" while others (Gentiles) would "recline at the table with Abraham, Isaac, and Jacob in the kingdom of heaven." (We probably will never appreciate how truly offensive this sounded to the Jews who heard it.)

This means that being a *son* of the kingdom (one who was first to be invited, and who naturally should have honored that invitation) did not always guarantee *entrance* into it. The privilege of being the first group God invited was a good thing, but with privilege comes responsibility. Jesus did not seek mere accredited candidates for the kingdom; He sought those whose hearts were already seeking the kingdom. This is why John the Baptist said to them, "Therefore bear fruit in keeping with repentance; and do not suppose that you can say to yourselves, 'We have Abraham for our father'; for I say to you that from these stones God is able to raise up children to Abraham" (Mat. 3:8–9). Being "children of Abraham" is not what qualified the Jews to be in God's kingdom but love for and obedience to His Son.

It is tragic—and condemnable—that when Pilate tried to release Jesus, declaring (whether sincerely or sarcastically is hard to tell) that He was their King, the Jews replied, "We have no king but Caesar!" (John 19:15). This was the Jews' ultimate betrayal of their King: they chose a ruler whom they hated and who oppressed them over a King who had done no wrong and worked miracles among them. Then they chose a robber, insurrectionist, and murderer named Barabbas to be released instead of Jesus (Mark 15:7–15). With these two awful decisions, the Jews to whom God had promised first entrance into His kingdom (Acts 3:25–26) rejected that offer and murdered their own King.

The second usage of "sons of the kingdom" also applies to the Jews, though Christians today often use it to refer to themselves by extension. In His parable about the wheat and tares, Jesus said that the "sons of the kingdom" are "good seed" scattered throughout the world, bringing with them the message of redemption through Jesus Christ (Mat. 13:24–30, 36–43). These will have to contend with false teachers and false teachings (the "tares") but will be sown throughout the world anyway. We see the fulfillment of this teaching in early church history: the book of *Acts* describes how believing Jews (including the apostles themselves) "who had been scattered" by persecution in Jerusalem "went about preaching the word" (Acts 8:4).

This is, of course, a positive usage of "sons of the kingdom." These are Jewish men (and women) who internalized the message of the kingdom and sought to share it with the world. Jesus spoke of these people matter-of-factly, as if this were how it should have been, what He expected of His people, and the correct application of His teachings. These Jews did not assume a kingdom status based upon ethnicity or heritage but obedient faith in the King, and personal commitment to His moral principles. Gentile believers who embraced these principles would later join (and ultimately eclipse) their work.

Summary Thoughts: The message of the kingdom of God, as preached by Jesus in His earthly ministry, was not yet meant for the entire world to hear. It was designed for, spoken to, and required of the Israelite people, members of a national covenant that God had established under Moses' leadership. These were the people whom Jesus taught; this was His initial target audience. In His own words, "I must preach the kingdom of God to the other cities [besides Capernaum] also, for I was sent for this purpose" (Luke 4:43, bracketed words are mine).

In His personal self, His teachings, and His miracles, Jesus fulfilled the OT prophecies concerning the Messiah. No one with an open mind—then or now—should be able to read these prophecies without seeing Jesus written all over them. This is not the result of "Christian conditioning," in which Christians "see" Jesus in these writings only because we want Him to fit our profile of the NT Messiah. Rather, anyone can observe this on his own; the Scriptures speak for and can defend themselves well.

Jesus was the spiritual David and Branch of OT prophecy. He is the fulfillment of everything the prophets said and wrote concerning the coming Messiah, a personification of the idealized nation of Israel (thus, "Israel, My Servant"—Isa. 41:8). As Paul would later say, He is "the summing up of all things…in the heavens and on the earth" (Eph. 1:10), whatever God needed to be done *here* and in the spiritual realm.

The Jews followed Jesus in droves around the countryside, continually amazed by His teachings and miracles. They supposed that, if He were the Messiah, God was about to unveil His kingdom to the world and thus would subjugate Rome and all other nations. The fervor this created, while short-lived, dogged Jesus wherever He went, and His miracles only fanned the flames of excitement. But Jesus never once said that He was going to be an earthly king or reign in Jerusalem. He said the opposite: He will reign from heaven and would raze Jerusalem to the ground for refusing to welcome its King (Luke 19:41–44).

The "sons of the kingdom"—whether believers or unbelievers—refers to the Jews, the people of God by covenant. Some of these "sons" were obedient to the word and carried the message of Christ into the world after Christ's ascension. Others, however, refused to believe, or refused to do anything *about* their belief, and thus nullified their opportunity to enter the kingdom. What all Jews *should* have done—and had every reason to do it—was listen to Jesus' kingdom messages, believe in the God-anointed King, and strive to enter the kingdom itself.

These latter things are exactly what the gospel of Christ calls us to do: listen, believe, and strive to be obedient. While the original message was for the Jews, the message now is for all people everywhere.

Part Two

The Kingdom and Salvation

Chapter Five

The Purpose of Christ's Rule over the Kingdom

The kingdom of God, as it has been revealed to us through the Scriptures, is all about the redemption of human souls. The plan of this redemption is an "eternal purpose which He carried out in Christ Jesus our Lord" (Eph. 3:11), and God giving rule of His kingdom to Christ is a necessary part of that eternal purpose. The conception of this purpose precedes time, the Creation, and humanity (2 Tim. 1:9); its effects extend forward into the eternity to come. The kingdom has always been, but Christ has not always been its king; the kingdom will always be, but Christ will not always need to be its king.

So then, there is a purpose for why God made His Son the King over His own kingdom. And yet there is Paul's comment that at "the end," Christ will "[hand] over the kingdom to God the Father, when He has abolished all rule and authority and power" (1 Cor. 15:24).

There are two major things to consider here:

- **First**, Christ was the sole heir of His Father, so that whatever belonged to the Father was inherited by the Son. This speaks to the *rightfulness* of the transaction or Christ's *entitlement* as the Son of God.
- **Second**, there must be a specific reason for God to give His kingdom over to His Son, and then for His Son to give it back to His Father. This objective must have a beginning point (when Christ takes the throne) and an ending point (when He hands rule of the kingdom back to His Father). This speaks to the *purpose* of the transaction, which is important to us because God never does anything without a clear and known purpose. (This handing the kingdom back to the Father will be covered in a later chapter.)

The Heir of All Things: God the Father has one heir, and that is His Son—His "only begotten" (John 1:18, 3:16, and 1 John 4:9). "Only begotten" comes from a Greek word [*monogenes*] which means, "the only born"; a "sole child"; a "one-of-a-kind" (son).[46] In the event of an only child, that child legally becomes the sole heir of his father's estate.

While we are all made sons of God through faith, and through having been adopted by the Father into His household (Gal. 3:26–27, 4:4–7), we are not natural sons of God but of human beings. Jesus was conceived by the Holy Spirit (Luke 1:35), which is another way of saying that He was conceived by God. Because of this, He has a unique and unparalleled existence to all other people who have been born only of flesh and blood (Luke 1:31; compare John 1:12–13).

The *Hebrews* writer states Christ's entitlement directly: "in these last days He [God] has spoken to us in His Son [Christ], whom He appointed heir of all things" (Heb. 1:2a, bracketed words are mine).[47] Christ is "heir of all things"—that is, all things *created*, as the rest of Heb. 1:2 states—because He deserves this as God's only begotten Son. While Christ's spiritual church, which comprises the faithful of all time (all those redeemed by His blood), will inherit the kingdom of God in future glory, Christ's inheritance is a shared one. The redeemed do not *deserve* and are not *entitled* to such inheritance, but Christ will *share* His inheritance with them because they are members of His "body" (Col. 1:18).

God's transfer of responsibility was a legitimate transaction. Christ did not establish a kingdom of His own which would operate concurrently with or (worse) as a rival to God's eternal kingdom. There is and always has been only one kingdom of God; whatever Christ rules over now is what God has always ruled over forever. Christ is not a usurper of God's throne; He is not competing for this; He never does anything in conflict with or contradiction to this. "The Father loves the Son and has given all things into His hand" (John 3:35).

Christ's kingdom is still the *Father's* kingdom, but He oversees it in His own name. This is why He calls it "My kingdom," as in His conversation with Pontius Pilate (John 18:36).[48] At the same time, He recognizes His Father's full and immutable *ownership* of this kingdom, as we see in Mat. 26:29 ("I will not drink of this fruit of the vine until…in My Father's kingdom").

The point in which God made this legal transfer of power is when His Son was "exalted to the right hand of God" and formally recognized as the King over His Father's kingdom (Acts 2:33). This "right hand of God" position indicates that complete rule and authority have been given to the one who occupies it. We see this consistently and persistently in the NT:

- "But from now on the Son of man will be seated at the right hand of the power of God" (Luke 22:69, citing Psalm 110:1).
- "He is the one whom God exalted to His right hand as a Prince and a Savior, to grant repentance to Israel, and forgiveness of sins" (Acts 5:31).
- "[W]ho is the one who condemns? Christ Jesus is He who died, yes, rather who was raised, who is at the right hand of God, who also intercedes for us" (Rom. 8:34).
- "which [God] brought about in Christ, when He raised Him from the dead and seated Him at His right hand in the heavenly places" (Eph. 1:20).
- "Therefore if you have been raised up with Christ, keep seeking the things above, where Christ is, seated at the right hand of God" (Col. 3:1).
- "[Christ], having offered one sacrifice for sins for all time, sat down at the right hand of God" (Heb. 10:12).
- "fixing our eyes on Jesus, the author and perfecter of faith, who…has sat down at the right hand of the throne of God" (Heb. 12:2).
- "[Christ] is at the right hand of God, having gone into heaven, after angels and authorities and powers had been subjected to Him" (1 Peter 3:22).

Having received the kingdom from His Father, Christ the Son now exercises full and unlimited authority over all that has come into existence. With this authority He can provide redemption for human souls. God the Father, powerful as He is, cannot atone for sin on His own (apart from the mediative work of His Son). By giving all authority to His Son, the Father deals with two situations all at once: all souls, principalities, kingdoms, etc. that oppose Him; and those who seek salvation from divine condemnation for their sins.

This "right hand of God" position remains, however, a delegated authority since the kingdom was legally transferred and not taken by force or assumed. Christ states this in His resurrected instructions: "All authority has been *given to Me* in heaven and on earth" (Mat. 28:18, emphasis added). This means that God did not absolve Himself of all power and authority for His Son to reign; He still maintains His sovereign authority (see 1 Cor. 15:27–28). This does not mean there are two separate Kings ruling over a single kingdom. It means there is *one* King (Christ) who rules over His Father's kingdom in His (the Father's) name.

In this capacity, Christ the King will never do anything to violate, undermine, or usurp His Father's kingship or His kingdom. The two (Father and Son) work seamlessly together; Jesus said, "I and the Father are one" (John 10:30), indicating their divine unity and continual agreement (see John 17:20–23). Whatever God wants for His kingdom, Christ wants; any decision God makes for His kingdom, Christ makes that decision in His Father's name. There is no division, schism, disunity, rivalry, or competition.

This does not mean Christ is merely God's mouthpiece, or a mere figurehead with no power of His own. It means that all the power He does exercise will always be in full agreement with the power His Father has always exercised. This is like saying that the President has power to act with power and authority, but anything he does will be (ideally) in full agreement with the law of the land, the United States Constitution. Just as the President must never break the law (and took an oath of office to this end), so Christ will never break His Father's law, which is to say that He will never act or speak in any way that defies God. (This is also true because Christ, being also a divine Being, cannot defy *Himself*.) God never changes; He cannot deny His own divinity (2 Tim. 2:13). But Christ also never changes; He also cannot deny *His* own divinity (Heb. 13:8).

As King, Christ makes things happen. He governs the physical universe, holding everything together by His own power (Col. 1:17). He governs the spiritual universe, which refers to all angelic powers or principalities (Eph. 1:20–21). He renders decisions concerning His kingdom and the disposition of every human soul. Even wicked kingdoms (both earthly and spiritual) will answer to Him; He is not responsible for what they do, but He does *limit* what they can do and they will *give account* to Him for this. Christ is not a ceremonial King who occupies an official office but has no direct control over His kingdom (I am thinking of the king and queen of England, for example). Rather, He exerts direct and continuous power, authority, and influence over all that is under Him—which is the entire Creation.

The United Office of Priest and King: The other reason God gave all authority over all Creation to His Son is for the purpose of the redemption of human souls. In taking His position at the right hand of God, Christ also (simultaneously) took the position of a High Priest over His church. He concurrently serves as both *King* and *High Priest* of God's kingdom. No high priest of Israel ever sat on a throne; no king of Israel ever ministered as a high priest. Priests mediate, kings rule; priests work standing up (at the altar), kings work sitting down (upon a throne). The fact that our High Priest reigns on a throne as a great King indicates the merging of two offices into one (in fulfillment of Zech. 6:11–13).

This merging of the two into one is what is meant in Psalm 110:4: "The Lord has sworn and will not change His mind, 'You are a priest forever according to the order of Melchizedek.'" Melchizedek [Heb., *melchi*, "king" + *zedek*, "righteousness"[49]] was an ancient priest-king who ruled over Salem (Gen. 14:17–20), later known as Jerusalem (see Psalm 76:2).

His great distinction here is that he was both priest *and* king, a united office which we do not encounter in Scripture again until Christ (see Heb. 7:1–28).

This dual office is the reference point for "according to the order of." It does not mean that Christ inherited (or is a successor to) what Melchizedek began. Rather, it means that as Melchizedek was both priest and king, so Christ will be. The ancient priest-king's united role serves as a "type" prophecy—one that is demonstrated rather than spoken—for Christ's own role in His Father's kingdom.

These two offices, in the context of the redemption of human souls, work together. As the King, Christ has authority to pronounce a human soul *innocent* of its crimes against Him. This is what the process of justification is all about (see Rom. 5:1–2). Justification—the acquitting of moral crimes and (simultaneously) the reconciliation of a soul's fellowship with God—is a legal action. Priests do not render legal decisions; this is kingly work. When Christ exonerates a soul of its guilt, He does so with the authority He has as God's heir—as a King over God's kingdom. He does not need His Father's permission because He already has it: in giving His kingdom to His Son, God gave Him all the permissions necessary to operate in that capacity. The kingdom of God is also the kingdom of Christ (Eph. 5:5).

However, a king does not make *atonement* for sin because this is priestly work. And a king cannot legally pronounce innocence prior to atonement. Sin must be dealt with first, then restoration or reconciliation. Under the Law of Moses, the priests would both offer sacrifices of their own (for their own sins and for the sins of the nation) and receive sacrifices brought to them by the Israelites. They would put all these sin offerings upon the bronze altar in front of the tabernacle/temple as a propitiation to God (i.e., an appeasement of His wrath). The atonement technically was made through the blood of these sacrifices, but the priests were the official administrators of the entire sacrificial system.

In the case of Christ, He has offered Himself as a sin offering for all people for all time. (Again, this speaks to the availability of this offering, not the application of it.) He has not offered this according to the Law of Moses because this offering exceeds that context. "For the Law, since it has only a shadow of the good things to come and not the very form of things, can never, by the same sacrifices which they offer continually year by year, make perfect those who draw near" (Heb. 10:1). Because of this, "it is impossible for the blood of bulls and goats to take away sins" (Heb. 10:4).

But it *is* possible for Christ—through the offering of His body and blood—to take away sins. In fact, this was the purpose for His having provided Himself as a blood sacrifice: because of this, redeemed souls "have been sanctified through the offering of the body of Jesus Christ once for all" (Heb. 10:10). Through this unique and holy offering, human sins are expiated (atoned for), and the justice due those sinful souls is carried out in His death, on His cross.

This is where the two massive worlds of justice and atonement merge. In God's realm—which is the realm we should be most concerned with—justice cannot be ignored, but it can be diverted to someone other than the guilty party. Christ's life can be given for our life; "For Christ also died for sins once for all, the just for the unjust, so that He might bring us to God" (1 Peter 3:18).

> [T]he real and most profound explanation of the presence of the kingdom is to be sought in the person of Jesus Himself. The secret of the presence of the kingdom of heaven [i.e., in the seemingly present-tense way in which Jesus speaks of it] lies in Jesus' victory over Satan, in His unlimited miraculous power, His unrestricted authority to preach the gospel, in His pronouncements of blessedness and the bestowal of salvation upon His people.[50]

As for atonement, this is priestly work that requires a high priest of divine ordination that does not rest on human authority, human power, or a law that governs human beings (i.e., the Law of Moses). This is the point the *Hebrews* writer makes with reference to Christ's ordination: the Law could not have ordained Him as a priest because He did not meet the Law's credentials. He was not from the tribe of Levi, or a descendent of Aaron, which are required of priests by the Law. Rather, He was from the tribe of Judah, and an "only begotten Son" of God. It is for this reason that God declared His Son "a priest forever" by His own divine authority (an oath). "For the Law appoints men as high priests who are weak, but the word of the oath, which came after the Law, appoints a Son, made perfect forever" (Heb. 7:28).

God's Church: A natural question here might be, "Where do all these redeemed souls go?" or "What is the present state of redeemed souls (Christians)?" The answer is that they are all "added" to a visible community of believers (Acts 2:47), known as "the church." This "church" can be identified as a brotherhood of believers (without geographical distinction) or as a specific congregation in a specific city (compare Acts 9:31 and 1 Cor. 1:2, for example).[51] Many people think "the church" and "the kingdom of God" are identical or interchangeable, but this is incorrect and will be covered in detail later.

Christ is the builder of His church ("I will build My church"—Mat. 16:18), since it is, in a spiritual context, "His body" (Col. 1:18). Christ's "body" of believers serves as the sanctuary of those souls who are all put on equal status: as they once were all sinners (regardless of the nature, frequency, or duration of their sins), now they "are all one in Christ Jesus" (regardless of age, gender, ethnicity, or status) (Gal. 3:28). They "belong" to Christ (Gal. 3:29); He has "purchased [them] with His own blood" (Acts 20:28); they no longer give allegiance to sin (or "the world") but to their new Master (Rom. 6:8–20).

Even so, the spiritual church is identified as belonging to God six times in the NT.[52] It is identified as God's church in the physical (congregational) sense another four times.[53] Only once is there a stated reference to the church as belonging to Christ, and this is in the physical sense (Rom. 16:16). There is no contradiction here: as discussed earlier, whatever belongs to God belongs also to Christ (John 16:15). Yet, God maintains supreme authority over His Son, as indicated, for example, in Eph. 1:19–22:

- The strength of *God's* might was brought about through Christ.
- *God* raised Christ from the dead through *His* power.
- *God* seated Christ at His right hand.
- *God* placed Christ above all other authorities, powers, and dominions.
- *God* put Christ "as head over all things to the church."

God the Father is the one who initiated all these actions (i.e., brought about, raised, seated, placed, put). Christ did not appoint Himself as the head of His church any more than He appointed Himself as a king over God's kingdom or a high priest to God (Heb. 8:3).[54]

Therefore, those who belong to Christ also belong to God. Those who are in Christ's church ("His body") are also in God's church (see 1 Thess. 1:1, where Paul says that the Thessalonian Christians are in both God *and* Christ). Those in whom Christ dwells, God also dwells (1 John 2:24). No one can have fellowship with the Father without the Son, and no one can have fellowship with the Son without the Father (1 John 1:3). No one can come to the Son unless the Father draws him to Him (John 6:44), and no one can come to God except through the Son (John 14:6).

Summary Thoughts: In his defense before the Jewish Council, Peter said that Christ "is the one whom God exalted to His right hand as a Prince and a Savior, to grant repentance to Israel, and forgiveness of sins" (Acts 5:31). The exaltation to the right hand of God refers to His kingship; the forgiveness of sins refers to His work as a divine high priest. Both roles fulfill the purpose of God's having given His kingdom over to His Son; each role needs the other to save souls.

These two ideas, roles, and functions are brought together in Heb. 8:1: "Now the main point in what has been said is this: we have such a high priest, who has taken His seat at the right hand of the throne of the Majesty in the heavens…" Our sympathetic High Priest is also a sitting King. Through Him, our souls are atoned of their sins, and thus we are justified in God's court of law.

God is a God of justice, and that justice must be fulfilled in dealing with sin (i.e., atonement) as it is in making legal declarations (which is what "justification" is all about in the doctrine of salvation). Whoever then belongs to God also belongs to Christ, and vice versa. The Father is the source and possessor of salvation, but He could not have saved anyone without His Son's intercessory blood sacrifice.

As it is, God's kingdom with His perfect Son at its helm provides everything necessary for any person to come to God, be forgiven of his sins, and walk in fellowship with the King.

Chapter Six

Kingdom and Salvation: Two Sides of the Same Coin

"The time is fulfilled, and the kingdom of God is at hand; repent and believe in the gospel" (Mark 1:15). These are Jesus' first recorded words in Mark's gospel. In so speaking, He links the coming revelation of God's kingdom and the gospel message *of* that revelation. He does not make these two separate things but presents them as a singular message.

Thus, "the gospel [lit., good news]" of salvation is also the "gospel of the kingdom," a phrase used four times in the gospel accounts.[55] The kingdom, as Jesus preached it, has everything to do with salvation. But salvation itself rests upon God's power (Rom. 1:16), Jesus' kingship, and His role as the Redeemer. These things are interwoven in the "eternal purpose which He [God] carried out in Christ Jesus our Lord" (Eph. 3:11).

> Jesus spoke of the work of salvation as the kingdom or reign of heaven in order to indicate the supernatural character, origin, and purpose of our salvation. Our salvation begins in heaven and should redound [i.e., return] to the glory of the Father in heaven. Hence, by using this term Christ defended the truth, so precious to all believers, that everything is subservient to God's glory.[56]
>
> The development of the "kingdom of God" then runs parallel to the development of the "redemption story." Both themes involve each other. ... So redemption, royal authority, glory, forgiveness, and dominion all weave together in this unfolding eternal purpose of God.[57]

The kingdom and salvation are mutually dependent. Salvation is impossible without Jesus' sacrifice, resurrection, and exaltation to the right hand of God. Yet the kingdom under Christ is, apart from salvation, a mere ceremonial change and not a purposeful one, since nothing is really accomplished by it (for us, anyway). Jesus did not come to our world only to talk about kingships and kingdoms; He came, in His own words, "to seek and save the lost" (Luke 19:10). He also knew, better than we will ever know, that this required Him to be King.

Salvation Is the Objective: "Salvation" is one's state of being in a right relationship with God through having been atoned of sins by Christ's blood.[58] This is Christ's objective, to render salvation to those who choose to align themselves with the King (Himself), the kingdom's teaching, and fellow kingdom believers.

Alignment implies agreement and conformity rather than mere identification. Identity is different from conformity. Many people today, for example, identify as "Christians" but do not agree or conform with Christ, His teachings, and His church. No one becomes right with God through names, church attendance, or even good intentions (Mat. 7:21–23, Titus 1:15–16).

Whenever Jesus spoke of the kingdom of God, He most certainly implied that He would be its King, and that through His kingship He would bring salvation to the world. He is not only the King of the Jews—the fulfillment of messianic prophecies given *to* the Jews concerning God's relationship with their nation—but also over the entire Creation.

However, He is not saving every Jew, since salvation is determined by one's personal faith in His kingship, not one's ethnicity. He is not saving all of Creation, either, because He died to save human souls, not a corrupted system. On the other hand, His salvation of believers does render the entire Creation worthwhile,[59] in that it provides God what He wanted all along: those who choose to worship Him above all else.

In referencing God's kingdom, Jesus consistently pointed us to the source of this salvation. It is not in Greek or Roman philosophy, or any human philosophy that has come about since then. It is not in

Judaism, which emphasized law-keeping even above righteousness, thus missing the point altogether (Rom. 10:2–4). It is not in other *forms* of law-keeping, such as what is often preached and practiced in Christian churches today. It is not in churches, preachers, sermons, or pious living. Instead, salvation is inherently, directly, and exclusively from God.

> Jesus spoke of the work of salvation as the kingdom or reign of heaven in order to indicate the supernatural character, origin, and purpose of our salvation. Our salvation begins in heaven and should redound [i.e., return] to the glory of the Father in heaven. Hence, by using this term Christ defended the truth, so precious to all believers, that everything is subservient to God's glory.[60]

Remember that Jesus preached the kingdom/salvation to Jews who for centuries had been conditioned to believe that they could earn their way to heaven by keeping the Law of Moses. The Law itself does state this: "So you shall keep My statutes and My judgments, by which a man may live if he does them; I am the Lord [Jehovah]" (Lev. 18:5). What God meant here was that if any person kept His Law perfectly, then it would justify him as a righteous man. There would be no need for mercy, grace, or forgiveness, since these are gifts for sinners, not perfect people. Ideally, this was to be the case: every Israelite man who received circumcision was to keep God's Law perfectly (Gal. 5:3).

This, of course, never happened—with Jesus Christ being the only exception. He is the only Man to ever live who has kept God's law perfectly (1 Peter 2:22). Thus, He and He alone is justified by law; the rest of the Jews—and every other person who has ever lived—all sinned, fell short of God's holiness, and needed forgiveness through some means *apart* from law. (This does not render law unnecessary; it only reveals its limitation. Law teaches how we can be forgiven but cannot impart forgiveness; it explained what must be done to justify a lawbreaker but cannot produce the justification.)

By Jesus' day, the Jewish leadership had beaten the heads of all Jews with the club of law-keeping as a means of righteousness. The better you keep the laws, the closer you are to God; thus, the Jewish leaders taught the Law was, in essence, a merit system (Rom. 10:2–4). This trivialized the blood sacrifices, since it was through blood that God granted atonement (Lev. 17:10–11), not penance or human attempts to work off sin through law-keeping. The Jewish leadership—the elders, scribes, priests, and ecclesiastic officials—believed that if a few laws were good, then more laws must be better. Thus, they added their laws to God's and then treated the two bodies of law as though God required them both. (In Mat. 15:1–9, for example, Jesus condemns this.)

To be clear, Jesus' preaching did not shy away from law (or, the Law). He never undermined or negated the importance of keeping commandments.[61] Anyone who did so, He said, "shall be called least in the kingdom of heaven" (Mat. 5:17–19), which is another way of saying that God will not honor him.[62] Jesus did, however, have divine knowledge and wisdom by which He could interpret and apply law (as a judge or arbiter) with perfect justice. This explains His "you have heard it said…but I say to you" statements in His sermon on the mount (Mat. 5:21ff).

But Jesus also recognized that law is not the answer to human sin. The objective for Jesus' kingship was not to legislate more laws (either different ones or the increase of them) but a once-for-all means by which to deal with sin, thus reconciling human souls with the God who created them. The kingdom of God itself would become a "law" to those who submitted to it and gave their allegiance to its King. But being a citizen of the kingdom would also give that person access to divine mercy, grace, and forgiveness.

This access is vitally important to us. The Israelite people never had access to God except through the priesthood. And even the priests had no access to the innermost sanctuary of the temple (the Holy of Holies—Exod. 26:33) except the high priest, and then only once a year (on the Day of Atonement—see Lev. 16). Israelites could draw near to God by faith, but this was a faith predicated upon and maintained by their devotion to the four elements of worship: the Law, priesthood, sacrificial system, and tabernacle/temple.

The kingdom of God under Christ changed all this. It provided direct access—through prayer and faith—to the King, who is also our "great high priest who has passed through the heavens, Jesus the Son of God" (Heb. 4:14). Three significant passages highlight this access:

- "Therefore, having been justified by faith, we have peace with God through our Lord Jesus Christ, through whom also we have obtained our introduction by faith into this grace in which we stand; and we exult in hope of the glory of God" (Rom. 5:1–2). The word "introduction" here comes from the same Greek word elsewhere translated "access."[63] We have access *by* faith *into* grace. This is possible only through Jesus' kingship and high-priestly mediation.
- "And He [Jesus] came and preached peace to you who were far away, and peace to those who were near; for through Him we both have our access in one Spirit to the Father" (Eph. 2:17–18). The "near" are the Jews; the "far away" are Gentiles. Both groups are brought into "one new man" (2:15) in the sanctuary of the church, which Christ built with His regal authority.
- "This [mystery now revealed—MY WORDS] was in accordance with the eternal purpose which He carried out in Christ Jesus our Lord, in whom we have boldness and confident access through faith in Him" (Eph. 3:11–12). Paul uses three terms here: "Christ," "Jesus," and "Lord." "Christ" refers to Jesus' role as the Redeemer, the One promised to the world through the OT prophets. "Jesus" refers to His human manifestation ("the Word became flesh"—John 1:14). "Lord" speaks to His royal authority as the King of God's kingdom. He does not "reign" over His church but is indeed its Savior, head, Shepherd, and Guardian (Eph. 5:23, Col. 1:18, and 1 Peter 2:25).

Now, because Christ has taken His seat at the right hand of God *and* entered the heavenly tabernacle where God dwells, we have access to salvation (Heb. 8:1–2). This "new and living way"—think of "way" as access, not just method—is possible only through the blood sacrifice of our "great priest" (Heb. 10:19–21). The only one who could give us access to the Father is His Son; "no one comes to the Father but through Me" (John 14:6).

We no longer must pilgrimage to a holy temple, offer animals on an altar for atonement, or rely upon an earthly priesthood to intercede for us. Christ's church/body *is* the temple; Christ is our once-for-all sacrifice (Heb. 10:10); Christ is our priestly mediator (1 Tim. 2:5); and His kingdom expectations is our law. Christ the King is God's answer to our fallen world, including our own personal fallenness.

> After Jesus had returned to heaven, the apostles did not continue to make the kingdom the central theme of their preaching. Instead, they began to speak of eternal life, salvation, forgiveness, and other themes. In doing this, they were not deserting Jesus' concern for the kingdom of God. They were simply expressing the same idea in their way. To speak of salvation is to speak of the kingdom. We might express it as follows: God is graciously giving salvation as a free gift (extending His kingdom) to anyone who will receive it (enter the kingdom) through His Son Jesus Christ, and this salvation begins now (the kingdom is in the midst of you) and will be completed in the future (the kingdom will come like a thief in the night).[64]

This is what the kingdom of God is all about: offering salvation to those alienated from God because of sin. This is what the kingdom has *always been* about, long before Jesus was ever born as a Man. Everything in the OT sets the stage for and points forward to this objective. God, because of His great love for us, put a plan in motion from eternity to "to redeem us from every lawless deed, and to purify for Himself a people for His own possession, zealous for good deeds" (Titus 2:14). Christ accomplished all this through His incarnation, ministry, death, resurrection, ascension, and exaltation to the throne of God. "Our responsibility is not to save the world. ... However, we have a message of power to take to the world. It is the Gospel of the Kingdom."[65]

Allegiance to the King: Through His grace, Christ has done for us what we could never have done for ourselves. The essential definition *of* grace is whatever God does that we are unable to do for our own salvation. Forgiveness of sins is part of that divine gift, but it is not the entirety of it. God's grace illuminates, teaches, and transforms us in ways that we cannot understand yet can experience in the form of spiritual growth, maturity, and wisdom.[66]

But salvation is not a one-party or one-sided transaction. While the kingdom provides for salvation, God does not save anyone who refuses to give his allegiance to its King. In this allegiance, a person voluntarily chooses to make Christ his Lord—the King of his heart—and submits to His authority over all other authorities. Scripture never refers to Christ as "the King of His church" because He does not reign over His church as He does all Creation. On the other hand, each member *of* His church must honor and obey Christ as Lord over all things. Christians do this voluntarily; in time, "every knee will bow" to Him at God's command, "those who are in heaven and on earth and under the earth" (Phil. 2:9–10).

The Jews of Jesus' day who did not receive Him as their King forfeited the salvation He offered them through His kingship. "He came to His own, and those who were His own did not receive Him. But as many as received Him, to them He gave the right to become children of God, even to those who believe in His name, who were born, not of blood nor of the will of the flesh nor of the will of man, but of God" (John 1:11–13).

Obviously, some Jews did receive Jesus as their King. These people likely did not understand His ministry as we do now (with the benefit of hindsight), but they believed in Him and surrendered to Him. Others identified Him as a King but did not follow Him ("Why do you call Me, 'Lord, Lord,' and do not do what I say?"—Luke 6:46). Still others rejected His claims of kingship altogether, even though He backed up these claims with many and profound miracles.

Jesus openly called out these two latter groups: "I have come in My Father's name, and you do not receive Me; if another comes in his own name, you will receive him. How can you believe, when you receive glory from one another and you do not seek the glory that is from the one and only God?" (John 5:43–44). Jesus cannot help those who will not receive Him; He cannot save those who refuse to acknowledge His kingship and obey Him as their King.

For this reason, Jesus said to these people, "You are from below, I am from above; you are of this world, I am not of this world. Therefore I said to you that you will die in your sins; for unless you believe that I am {He}, you will die in your sins" (John 8:23–24). The latter "I am" reference here (the "He" is not in the original Greek text) recalls God's own self-existence (see Exod. 3:14), in which Jesus asserts His divinity. But it also implies His mission as the Christ (Redeemer) by His authority as the Son of God. To believe that Jesus is the "I am" is to receive Him as the King whom God sent into the world as a solution to the problem of human sin. Specifically, it is the solution to our sins.

To receive Christ as King, one must give up his own kingdom first. This is what self-denial is all about: relinquishing one's control for the sake of receiving Christ's control (Mat. 16:24). To "save" oneself is to exercise his own control over his life; to "lose" one's life is to give control of it to Christ (Mat. 16:25). When we are sinners, sin is our master: sin controls us, whether we acknowledge or are aware of it. When we become Christians, Christ (ideally) is our Master—the King of our heart (Rom. 6:16). Christ is the King regardless of our allegiance to Him, but He cannot be *your* King or *my* King until you or I receive Him *as* King in every respect. If we do so, then God will receive us: His reception is based upon ours. If we refuse to do this, God will refuse to have fellowship with us: His rejection is based upon ours.

"No one can serve two masters; for either he will hate the one and love the other, or he will be devoted to one and despise the other. You cannot serve God and wealth" (Mat. 6:24). While Jesus specified "wealth" as a type of god in one's heart, we can replace this word with anything to which we give greater allegiance than Christ. Thus, "wealth" can be spouse, children, family, friends, status, power, a lifestyle or behavior, an addiction, etc. Regardless, "No one can serve two masters"—no one can have two kings with equal control, both receiving equal allegiance.

One will always be favored over the other; one will always become expendable at the request of the other. Christ will not share His kingship with any other king, just as God will not share His glory with any other god or idol (see Exod. 20:3–5).

Summary Thoughts: The gospel of Christ is the gospel of the kingdom. These are not two different messages but the same. Christians tend to emphasize "church" in their preaching of the gospel yet put little if any emphasis on "kingdom." This is the product, no doubt, of tradition, conditioning, and misunderstanding. If one obeys the gospel of Christ, he becomes a Christian; if he obeys the gospel of the kingdom, he becomes a Christian. This does not make "the church" and "the kingdom" equal but only the *message* that involves them both.

The Jews focused on laws, law-keeping, and justification by law with respect to their salvation. Some Christians do this as well, even as they talk and sing about grace, God's power, and the work of the Spirit. These two mindsets run contradictory to each other. It is true that all followers of Christ have laws (commandments) to keep; Christ said so Himself (John 14:15).

However, it is not true that citizenship in the kingdom of God merely trades one outdated set of laws for a new upgraded set. Laws are necessary, but so is grace. Kingly authority is necessary but so is high-priestly intercession. We must never grab hold of one side of this at the expense of the other.

Our allegiance to the King—which involves our adoration of Him as our Savior—is necessary if He is to save us. There is no greater authority that exists, save the Father Himself, than that of Jesus Christ. Yet despite such authority, He will not override our own free will. He calls us to voluntarily consent to relinquish our own will to accept His. This works in His best interest as well as ours. We give Him the moral, ethical, and legal permission to oversee our lives as He determines is best rather than forge our own path. He cannot be our Master if we insist on co-mastering with Him.

It is at this point that something needs to be said about differentiating between the kingdom of God and the church of God. This will be our next topic of discussion.

Chapter Seven

The Kingdom and the Church

As a much younger Christian, I was commonly taught that the kingdom of God was the same as Christ's spiritual church. Maybe you were taught this as well. It is still a popular teaching and even seems validated by certain NT passages.

Back then, I was convinced of this teaching; now, not at all. What changed? Better information. A clearer understanding of God's "eternal purpose." Refusing any longer to cram "church" into passages that talk about "kingdom" (and vice versa). Salvation is the common goal to both the kingdom and Christ's church, but just because two things have the same goal does not make them the same thing. A father and mother can have the same goal for their child, but this does not make the two parents the same person.

This discussion can be a bit challenging, not because of the difficulty of the material but because of people's resistance to the topic. Years of tradition, conditioning, and well-loved preachers have led people to believe a certain conclusion; this "new" position may appear virtually heretical in comparison. I ask that you approach this subject as you should with any other spiritual subject: with an open mind, open heart, and open Bible. We are in pursuit here of a better understanding, not a traditional one. We want to let Scripture defend itself, not seek to defend our traditions with our "take" on Scripture.

First Things First: It should be conspicuous up front that almost nowhere in His ministry does Jesus talk about His church, but He has a great deal to say about His kingdom. There are two exceptions to this: when He said, "I will build My church" (Mat. 16:18); and when He passively mentioned "the church" (as in, "tell it to the church") as a means of disciplining an unrepentant member (Mat. 18:17). But Jesus could not build His church until the Father enthroned Him at His right hand; thus, Jesus spoke of building His church in anticipation of this, not as a present reality. And "the church" to a Jew living under the Law of Moses was simply his Jewish congregation, assembly, or synagogue. It had no direct reference to Christ's church but only to the Jews' churches.

Think about what Jesus often said: "the kingdom of God is at hand"; "The kingdom of heaven can be compared to"; "To what shall we liken the kingdom of God?" etc. He never said, "The church is at hand"; He never offered a parable or other illustration about the church. His emphasis was upon the kingdom, not the church. The Jews were not expecting their King to build a church; they were expecting Him to reign over His kingdom. They had not been waiting for hundreds of years for a church to save their nation, but for a Davidic King and His kingdom. When someone said or did something that got Jesus' attention, He never said, "You are not far from the church" but "not far from the kingdom" (Mark 12:34).

As stated previously, believing in the gospel of the kingdom of God does not lead a person in a different direction than if he believes in the gospel of Christ. These are not two different gospels but two sides of the same one. One side focuses on Jesus' kingship, the heavenly and spiritual nature of His kingdom, and the moral obligations of those who become citizens of His kingdom. The other side focuses on Christ as the Savior of human souls, emphasizing His sacrificial death, atoning blood, and personal virtue as One who is worthy to save us.

But this does not make the kingdom equal to the church. (By "church" in this discussion, I am referring to the universal and spiritual body of the redeemed, not congregations or collections of congregations.) The kingdom is about authority, power, justice, and legal propriety. The church is about Christ personally, which is why Paul defines it as His "body" (Col. 1:18). It is the sanctuary of those cleansed by His blood and guided by His leadership.

These two things are deeply related: the church could not have been built apart from Jesus' kingdom authority; and His kingdom serves no good purpose in the salvation of souls if no one is saved. Given God's "eternal purpose" (Eph. 3:11), the kingdom needs the church, and the church needs the kingdom.

But sequentially, the kingdom is of primary importance. God had promised David an eternal throne upon which would sit one of His descendants. Through the prophets, God also promised the Jews a Davidic King (Messiah) and a new kingdom under His rule. This had to be carried out: the throne of David could not be vacant, and the oracles of the prophets could not be unfulfilled. (I covered all this in chapter two.)

In a much bigger picture, God had been disclosing His kingdom to the world since the beginning of humanity. Christ's church did not fulfill God's promise to Abram (*a.k.a.* Abraham) that "in you all the families of the earth will be blessed" (Gen. 12:3), but Christ did. This fulfillment resulted in the church being built but the church is not why people are blessed—it is not the source of divine blessings. Jesus was a descendant of Abraham as well as a descendant of David: by Him the entire human race has been blessed, and in Him the throne of David has become an eternal throne overseeing an eternal kingdom. (I covered this in chapter two as well.) His kingship over God's kingdom is the source of blessing for "all the families of the earth."

However, Christ's reign as King is not limited to those who have become part of His church. His reign oversees the entire Creation—anything and anyone that has come into existence—both in the physical and spiritual realms. When we say that His church is equal to (or the same thing as) His kingdom, we reduce His kingship to having oversight only over one relatively small group of people but no one else. We make Him as a King over His church—a claim or designation found nowhere in the NT. We also leave unanswered: if He is King only over His church, then who is king over everything else? Did the Father only give His Son *part* of His kingdom or all of it?

Traditionally, we have responded to this problem by saying, "No, Christ is also King over all things in heaven and on earth," and cite (correctly) Mat. 28:18. But if Christ's kingdom *is* the church, then He is only King *of* the church. And if His church is the same as His kingdom, then His kingdom is only as big as His church. In other words, we start tripping over ourselves trying to rectify something that was based upon a false premise to begin with.

On the other hand, if Christ is King over all things, as He said He is, then we recognize that the church is a subset of what He reigns over and not the entirety of it. "For by Him all things were created, both in the heavens and on earth, visible and invisible, whether thrones or dominions or rulers or authorities—all things have been created through Him and for Him" (Col. 1:16). This includes the church (Col. 1:18) but is not limited to it. Christ created all non-church things, and when the fullness of time came, He also created (built) His church.

Regarding this, here are some things to consider:

- The kingdom has always been in existence; the church has not. The physical Creation has been in existence longer than the church has, even though the church will be ushered into glory but not the physical Creation (as implied in Rev. 21:1–2).
- The church is a subset of (and thus subordinate to) the kingdom of God, not synonymous with it. All those who become members of Christ's church/body were already subjects of Christ's universal kingdom. What changed was not the kingdom or the church but the allegiance of those members to the King of kings rather than the god of this world (2 Cor. 4:3–4). (See the following discussion on this change of allegiance.)
- Jesus never preached that the church was "at hand," but only focused on the kingdom. His authority as King over God's kingdom had to be established first. The Jews were expected to recognize Jesus as *their* King so that they could be "sons of the kingdom" indeed.
  - While the Jews would be the first to inherit the kingdom, they would not be the only people to do so. In time, the Holy Spirit would invite Gentiles to become citizens of the kingdom as well (Acts 10).
  - "Jesus employed the phrase 'kingdom of God' or 'of heaven'

to indicate that perfect order of things which he was about to establish, in which all those of every nation who should believe in him were to be gathered together into one society, dedicated and intimately united to God, and made partakers of eternal salvation."[67]

- Jesus never equated His church with His kingdom, nor did any of His apostles. That there is a direct relationship between the two is indisputable: one cannot function without the other; to be "in the kingdom" (as Jesus meant this) is to be in His church (as Paul would later teach).
    - But the relation of two things does not make them the same thing; correlation is different from equality. My mom and dad were related by marriage, but they remained different people; my sister and I are related as siblings, but we are different people. There is an overlap in these concepts, to be sure: marriage is the overlap of a husband and wife; family is the overlap of siblings. Likewise, salvation is the overlap of Christ's kingdom and His church. All things pertaining to salvation are as important in His kingdom as they are in His church.
    - "While the term 'church' is not always co-extensive with the term 'kingdom,' the terms have nonetheless been **interrelated** since the church was established. Christ promised, 'I will build My church… I will give you [Peter] the keys of the kingdom' (Mat. 16:18–19). Seeing the interrelationship of the church and the kingdom will enable one to understand that with the establishment of the church came the full realization [or, purpose] of the kingdom of Old Testament prophecy, the reign of God through His Christ."[68]
- Jesus did not die for His kingdom, but He most certainly did die for His church (Eph. 5:2, 25). His sacrifice on the cross was not for the kingdom but His church. All souls who are under Christ's kingdom authority are not saved by His death, but all faithful souls who are in His church ("in Christ") most certainly are (Rom. 8:1).
- Jesus built His church within His Father's kingdom; He did not build them both. His Father's kingdom has always existed, but He (Jesus) has not always been its King. In His capacity as the

King, He exercised kingly authority to build His church. He never had authority to build—or rebuild, redesign, etc.—His Father's kingdom.

- Jesus was the heir of His Father's kingdom; He did not inherit His church. As stated earlier, the church came subsequent to the kingdom. His kingship is what God *gave* to Him because He is the "only begotten" Son of God and thus the heir of all things (Heb. 1:2). God did not build the church and then bequeath it to His Son; His Son built the church in God's name and God thus named His Son as its head (Eph. 1:22–23).

- We are not baptized into the kingdom of God but into Christ's body, the church. It is the kingdom to which we pledge allegiance, but it is the church to which we are added. We are "baptized into His death" (Rom. 6:3)—and, again, Christ did not die for the kingdom but for His church. We honor this death when we are baptized in the likeness of it.

- The Jews were not "sons of the church" but "sons of the kingdom." They were not heirs of a church membership but were to become citizens of God's kingdom under the reign of their Messiah. This is why the first preaching of the gospel of Christ to the Jews (and Jewish blood relatives, the Samaritans) necessarily included the kingdom of God (Acts 8:12, 19:8, 20:25, 28:23, and 28:31).

- In John 3:3–5, it does appear that entering "the kingdom" requires being "born again" of water and God's Spirit (in the NT context of salvation, this means baptism and the Spirit's sanctification). Christ's church is not mentioned here, leading some to think that He *meant* the church when He said "the kingdom." But there are a number of things He did not mention related to becoming a Christian. We must keep in mind, too, the man He was talking to (Nicodemus) was a Jew who no doubt had questions of God's kingdom and not Christ's church—something of which he had no knowledge at the time.

- The full realization of the kingdom of God is, after Acts 2, presented as a future promise. In contrast, when anyone becomes a member of Christ's church, he does so in real and present time. If you are a Christian, you are in Christ's church right now; but you have not yet inherited the kingdom of God. This is promised to you (if you remain faithful to the King) but you have yet to receive it. Thus, to "enter the kingdom" is first done by faith, by giving allegiance to a King whom we have never met or seen. But its factual reality is presented to us in future tense (see Acts 14:22, 1 Cor. 6:9–10, 15:50, Gal. 5:21, Eph. 5:5, 2 Tim. 4:18, etc.). You are its heir, but the inheritance will only be given after you have proven faithfulness to the King "until death" (Rev. 2:10).

The King's Castle: The best illustration I know to describe the relationship between the kingdom and church is that of a castle in the middle of a huge medieval-like domain. The king of the land has given all his authority to his son, the prince, who is also the head of his castle. But the prince has a hugely different relationship with the members of his castle than with all the subjects of his kingdom. All who live in the prince's realm are under his authority; all who live in the prince's castle are also under his authority but are regarded differently by him (and they regard him differently as well). Those in his realm that are not in his castle are strangers to the king and his son; those who are in his castle are his family (consider John 8:31–35 here).

The castle is the sanctuary of the kingdom, not the kingdom in its entirety. The kingdom includes all subjects in all realms overseen by the king's son, the prince. The castle has within it only those who have a familial relationship with the son—his household (consider 1 Tim. 3:15 here). While he is known only as "the king" to strangers in his land, the son is known personally, intimately, and affectionately by his family as the head of his household.

But how does one become part of the prince's household? In this case, only by adoption to the prince's father. Those who give their full allegiance to the king are welcomed in as family. They are not related biologically, since only his son has this distinction; he is the only begotten son of the father. But these people are legally related to the king and are thus all heirs to (or sharers in) what the son has already inherited. Not coincidentally, a moat of water surrounds the castle and the only way to get into the castle is through the water (consider Gal.

3:26–27 here). Once inside the castle, these adopted family members—"sons of [the king] by faith"—conform to the will and nature of the king and his son.

What about those outside the castle? They remain under the king's authority and in time the prince, who has inherited this authority, will deal with them. The king invited all of them into his castle, but most refused this invitation or simply disregarded it. This incurs the wrath of the king, which will be carried out through the judicial decisions of his son, whenever the king says is the right time to do this.

Thus, we see a relationship between the kingdom and the household but not interchangeableness, correlation but not equality. The one is within the other; the kingdom is not within the church, but the church is within the kingdom. The king owns the entire realm, and he has given all authority to his son; his son, however, has "built" the church through the addition of every soul that gives his allegiance to the king *because* of the son. I realize this is not a perfect analogy, but it does offer a means by which to understand the subject more clearly.

Change of Allegiance: The often-cited proof-text for "the church = the kingdom" argument is Col. 1:13–14: "For He rescued us from the domain of darkness, and transferred us to the kingdom of His beloved Son, in whom we have redemption, the forgiveness of sins." Up front, it sounds like we are in one domain over which Christ has no authority, then we are "transferred" to another domain which is completely under His authority.

But we have already seen that Christ has authority over *all* domains (as stated only a few verses later, in Col. 1:15–17), including those that are wicked and filled with spiritual darkness, those that are overseen by wicked spiritual rulers (like Satan). This does not mean Christ is responsible for what happens in these domains, or for the decisions of those in them, only that they will answer to Him. For now, they are His enemies who He allows to exist until everything runs its course. In time, they will no longer be allowed to exist or have any power (1 Cor. 15:23–25).

So then, what does Paul mean here? He is not talking about a literal transfer of one's soul across the border of one domain into the realm of another. One's soul is not "transferred" in the sense that he previously was *not* under Christ's authority but now *is*. All souls are under Christ's authority; He has no right to judge us if we are not (Acts 10:42, Rom. 2:16, 2 Cor. 5:10, etc.). This means believers will be judged by Christ but so will all non-believers, and all without respect to earthly status (Rom. 2:5–11).

Paul is talking here (in Col. 1:13–14) about a change of allegiance. It is the same thing he talks about in Rom. 6:3–14 but now far more succinctly and with different terms. When a person becomes a sinner, he gives himself over to the domain of darkness—the carnal, sensual, satanic realm of wickedness. Whether he realizes it, his god is the god of this world. When that person hears and obeys the gospel of Christ, his allegiance is no longer given to the domain of darkness but to Christ. Sin is no longer his master; Christ is (see Acts 26:18). This transfer of allegiance changes his spiritual status—not by his own power, but most certainly by his own decision—and he becomes a child (son) of God by faith. The historical and public event that marks this change of allegiance is his baptism in water (Acts 2:38, Gal. 3:26–27, 1 Peter 3:21, etc.).

Paul is not speaking about the church here (in Col. 1:13–14), although it is implied in the full discussion. All who give their allegiance to the King are made members of His church. Yet Paul's point is to focus on authority and one's allegiance to it. What kind of authority does Christ have? Paul immediately goes on (in 1:15–17) to expound upon this. Does the domain of darkness have this authority? Absolutely not. That domain is subordinate to Christ's authority, as are all domains in existence. Paul's "domain" and "kingdom" terminology underscores all this.

To phrase "in the kingdom of His beloved Son" is not about a geographical or locational transfer. The language here speaks to one's pledged allegiance to the King Himself, thus becoming a loyal citizen of the King (rather than a rebellious subject).

All loyal citizens are added to the King's household (His church); rebellious subjects, though still under the King's rule, remain strangers to Him (Eph. 2:19). The language here is relational, not positional or locatable. "The kingdom is the rule of God, and the realm of His blessings; the Church is the people of the kingdom who have received it, who witness to it, and who will inherit it."[69]

What of those whose hearts remain loyal to the domain of darkness? In time, these will be judged for having rejected the truth that God revealed to the world through His Son, and especially the truth of His resurrection (see Acts 17:30–31, 2 Thess. 1:6–9, and 2:10–12). Recall here my castle illustration.

Summary Thoughts: The church is not the kingdom; the kingdom is not the church. However, it is accurate to say that the church is the sanctuary of the redeemed who are within the kingdom. Specifically, these redeemed people had to have already given their allegiance to the King, God's Son. By the Son's authority, these have been pardoned; but this pardon was made possible through His blood offering. If not for this offering, there could be no pardon. Christ would, in that case, still be King but we cannot be saved apart from His high-priestly role.

The kingdom and the church are related but not interchangeable. Salvation is what brings the two together; it is the overlapping of the two things. The Father's kingdom was given to His Son for the purpose of the redemption of human souls. The church is the spiritual assembly of those souls who are saved through this redemption. One (the kingdom) focuses on a soul's legal disposition before the King; the other (the church) focuses on a soul's right relationship to the King as a family member. Neither of these stands alone; they must be taken together.

I hope that my castle/domain illustration was helpful. It is a simple analogy that is not meant to be pressed beyond its intention. Sometimes simple analogies are exactly what we need to cut through the blurriness of our own thoughts and understand the more technical details.

Next, we will see the kingdom authority and church assembly come together in a biblical presentation.

Chapter Eight

Mount Zion and New Jerusalem

Six hundred years before Christ, Babylon's expansionist and empire-building King Nebuchadnezzar invaded the nation of Judah. He carried into captivity Jewish scholars, artisans, military leaders, men of valor—all the leading men, including the young men of high intelligence (2 Kings 24:10–16).

Daniel was one of these young and extraordinary men. Nebuchadnezzar had him trained to serve in his court alongside his wise men and magicians (Dan. 1:1–7). Soon thereafter, Nebuchadnezzar had a perplexing dream that both astonished and disturbed him. He called for his native Chaldean wise men and magicians (soothsayer priests) and demanded an interpretation of his dream. Yet, he made one difficult stipulation: they had to tell him the dream themselves (to prevent any deception) and *then* interpret it (Dan. 2:1–12).

The wise men told the king that what he asked was humanly impossible; only a god is capable of this. Nebuchadnezzar took this as a means for them to save their own necks and called for the execution of all the wise men, conjurers, and magicians—which included Daniel and his three friends. Daniel prayed for God's help, then went to King Nebuchadnezzar and told him that he could interpret the dream (Dan. 2:13–30).

The Four-Kingdom Statue: The young Jewish man Daniel then went on to tell the king what his dream was—something that no one had ever done. In his dream, the king saw a great statue made of differing metals: a head of gold, breast and arms of silver, belly and thighs of bronze, legs of iron, and feet of mixed iron and clay. He went on to reveal that Nebuchadnezzar (and Babylon by extension) was the head of gold, an "inferior kingdom" was silver, another kingdom was bronze, and the fourth kingdom was iron (and, in the feet, iron mixed with clay).

This was historically fulfilled: after Babylon, the Medo-Persians ruled the world; after them, Greece; and finally, the Romans. The statue represented a four-fold kingdom of men, made and sustained by men, and as each kingdom faded from power it was absorbed into the next kingdom (except for Rome). Yet, while the size and power of each empire increased over time, its value or quality deteriorated: a golden kingdom would eventually be swallowed up by a kingdom of common iron.

In the dream, a "stone was cut without hands" and cast against, struck, and pulverized the metal statue into dust. This brought an end to this four-empire Gentile kingdom. (The number four in Scripture often refers to things related to the physical world, based upon the four elements: earth, water, fire, and wind. Thus, the four nations implied a man-made earthly power.) This "stone" then "became a great mountain that filled the whole earth" (Dan. 2:35).

While the metal statue was the product of human effort and sustained by human power and resources, the "stone" was otherworldly. The fact that it was "cut out without hands" implies that this was from heaven, not from earth (compare Mark 14:58, Col. 2:11, and Heb. 8:2). This was not something that came from men, was designed by men, or rested on human strength. This stone which became a mountain would not be succeeded by or absorbed into yet another stone or mountain but would become an everlasting kingdom. The statue of men could not be sustained; a single but powerful stone destroyed it. This stone-turned-mountain, however, would be invincible, overcoming all other kingdoms, destroying even the most powerful kingdom the world had ever seen: the Roman Empire.

Christ's Kingdom—the Stone-turned-Mountain: Most Bible students are familiar with this account. We realize the historical and prophetic importance of Nebuchadnezzar's dream and Daniel's interpretation of it. Many Christians, however, interpret the stone-turned-mountain to be Christ's church, but that is not what Daniel said. He revealed a kingdom, not a church; He prophesied about the revelation of God's power throughout the earth, not the work of believers and their congregations. "In the days of those kings [i.e., the fourth kingdom—Rome] the God of heaven will set up a kingdom which will never be destroyed, and that kingdom will not be left for another people; it will crush and put an end to all these kingdoms, but it will itself endure forever" (Dan. 2:44, bracketed words are mine).

> Relying principally on the prophecies of Daniel who had declared it to be the purpose of God that, after four vast and mighty kingdoms had succeeded one other and the last of them shown itself hostile to the people of God, at length its despotism should be broken, and the empire of the world pass over forever to the holy people of God. The Jews were expecting a kingdom of the greatest felicity, which God through the Messiah would set up, raising the dead to life again and renovating earth and heaven; and that in this kingdom they would bear sway forever over all the nations of the world. This kingdom was called the kingdom of God or the kingdom of the Messiah; and in this sense must these terms be understood in the utterances of the Jews and of the disciples of Jesus when conversing with them.[70]

God once dispersed the mass of human energy that devoted itself to building a great tower in Babel by confounding their languages (Gen. 11:1–9). Many centuries later, human energy went even further and devoted itself to building a great statue—a succession of empires that would rule over the known world. God let this continue only until it fulfilled His own purpose, which was to reveal His own kingdom to the world of humankind, then He would destroy that man-made kingdom completely.

"And Jesus came up and spoke to them, saying, 'All authority has been given to Me in heaven and on earth'" (Mat. 28:18). His Father had given the reins of His kingdom to His Son, so that He (the Son) would have authority over all things save for the Father Himself (1 Cor. 15:27–28). When Jesus rose from the dead, then rose to heaven, and then enthroned at the right hand of God—a three-fold exaltation—He soon put an end to the four-nation conglomerate empire. No longer would a single human kingdom or nation rule the entire world.

At the seventh trumpet in the revelation given to John, "there were loud voices in heaven, saying, 'The kingdom of the world has become the kingdom of our Lord and of His Christ; and He will reign forever and ever'" (Rev. 11:15). "And the nations were enraged" at this (11:18)—really, all the nations that Rome had absorbed from prior empires—and declared war not on Christ, but on His people. In the end, however, they found themselves fighting not against His church but against Christ Himself. This battle would end in doom for Rome.

We need to come back to the stone-turned-mountain imagery, however. Before Christ could build His church, it was necessary that He receive the authority to do so. Later in Daniel's life, God showed him a heavenly vision of Christ receiving this authority:

> I kept looking in the night visions, and behold, with the clouds of heaven One like a Son of Man was coming, and He came up to the Ancient of Days and was presented before Him. And to Him was given dominion, glory and a kingdom, that all the peoples, nations and men of every language might serve Him. His dominion is an everlasting dominion which will not pass away; and His kingdom is one which will not be destroyed. (Dan. 7:13–14)

This is an explanation of the stone-turned-mountain. What Daniel saw was Jesus (the "stone") receiving the kingdom ("a dominion") of His Father, the "Ancient of Days" (see Dan. 7:9–10). Jesus would be presented to the world as a seemingly small and insignificant stone—one that could easily be disposed of, the Jewish leaders assumed—yet His kingship would reign over all Creation, and the message of His kingdom would permeate the entire world.

Jesus the Cornerstone: We get another glimpse of this in Isaiah's prophecy: "Therefore thus says the Lord God, 'Behold, I am laying in

Zion a stone, a tested stone, a costly cornerstone for the foundation, firmly placed. He who believes in it will not be disturbed'" (Isa. 28:16). Here we have a three-fold identity of Christ's authority:

- **cornerstone for the foundation**—lit., a stone firmly placed or well-laid. This speaks to Christ's permanent and absolute authority. A cornerstone gives a structure stability, levelness, and orientation to its surroundings. It becomes a point of reference for whatever is built upon it. The paradox here is that natural stones do not grow but only shrink with time, erosion, or pulverization. A *living* stone defies all natural expectations; it is unnatural, or supernatural; it is not of this world but is otherworldly in its origin, design, and purpose.
- **tested stone:** one that has been tried, proven, and found worthy—in this case, to fulfill God's "eternal purpose" (Eph. 3:11), the universal plan of salvation. Thus, Jesus had to be "tempted in all things…yet without sin" (Heb. 4:15); He had to prove to God—and to the Jews, and to us—that He was intrinsically trustworthy, virtuous, and flawless. Even under the greatest duress—whatever pain and suffering (physical and otherwise) He experienced on the cross—He had to endure without failure. He "learned obedience through the things which He suffered" (Heb. 5:8), which does not mean that He learned *how* to be obedient (like we do, often through trial and error), but that He *experienced* obedience in His human state. As a result of His perfect success, He became a "faithful and true Witness" (Rev. 3:14), offering a permanent record in all history as One who was tested beyond all limits of human comprehension yet did not fail, fall, or sin.
- **costly [or, precious] stone**—referring to His intrinsic worth and divine character. He is priceless to us; His blood is priceless for the purpose of atoning for our sin (1 Peter 1:18–19). As "the Son of God's love" (Col. 1:18, in a literal translation), Christ is precious to God; as being "obedient in all things," He is precious to us. God did not entrust human salvation to a man (such as Peter), a group of men (clergy), or a collective of churches (a denomination). Rather, He tells us to listen to His Son since God now speaks to us through Him (Mat. 17:5, Heb. 1:1–2).

Permanence, stability, trustworthiness, integrity, preciousness—these are the foundational qualities which Christ exhibited to the world when He became flesh and dwelt among us. But these speak to His character and authority, not to His church. The foundation had to be laid *for* the church, and that foundation had to be correct (as a cornerstone), tested, and priceless. This foundation is what the church will be built upon so that it will not be shaken, moved, or destroyed. This is the "rock" (Mat. 16:18) upon which to build the sanctuary of redeemed souls; nothing less than this will suffice.

Zion and Jerusalem: In the OT messianic prophecies, "Zion" and "Jerusalem" are often mentioned together. We might assume that they are the same thing (as I did for years), but this is not the case. They are related but not equal; they are mutually dependent, not standalone ideas. Again, correlation does not mean equality. "Jerusalem"—not the literal city in Judea but the glorified city of God—cannot rest upon sand, earthly foundations, or human power. It must be built upon divine authority that comes directly from God Himself, since this city is His building (Heb. 11:16). Only this will be sufficient; only this will endure any evil assault, any human interference, and the ravages of time. "But as for Me," God said, "I have installed My King Upon Zion, My holy mountain" (Psalm 2:6).

"Zion" was once the symbolic name for the historical city of Jerusalem, dating back to the time of King David (2 Sam. 5:7, 9). Zion was an ancient fortress of the Jebusites, previous inhabitants of Jerusalem. David used this fortress for himself and referred to Jerusalem as the city of David. The hill of Zion is in the southeast end of ancient Jerusalem; Mt Moriah, where Solomon built the temple of God, was on another hill in the city to the north (2 Chron. 3:1). Moriah was either the place where Abraham was about to sacrifice Isaac (Gen. 22:2) or symbolizes this as a place of sacrifice.

Zion is the mountain; Jerusalem is the city. These are related but not the same: Zion is not Jerusalem and Jerusalem is not Zion. However, the *new* (messianic) Jerusalem will be built upon the *new* (messianic) Mt

Zion. The "mountain" archetype is common in history, literature, and religion. It signifies a place closest to the gods, closest to heaven, and transcendent of people. Mt Zion is no exception, eventually eclipsing Mt Sinai in theological importance.

> Now it will come about that in the last days the mountain of the house of the Lord will be established as the chief of the mountains, and will be raised above the hills; and all the nations will stream to it. And many peoples will come and say, "Come, let us go up to the mountain of the Lord, to the house of the God of Jacob; that He may teach us concerning His ways and that we may walk in His paths." For the law will go forth from Zion and the word of the Lord from Jerusalem. (Isa. 2:2–3)

Here we see both the glorified city (Jerusalem) *and* what it rests upon (Zion). Zion is the location of worship; Jerusalem is the people who worship there. Zion is not disconnected from the stone which became a mountain and covered the earth (from Dan. 2); it is the same thing. This "mountain" symbolizes the immovable and immutable authority of Christ upon which He will build His church. The city of David becomes (in the messianic prophetic context) the city of God, like a city "set on a hill" for the entire world and all humanity to see (Mat. 5:14).

> For Zion's sake I will not keep silent, and for Jerusalem's sake I will not keep quiet, until her righteousness goes forth like brightness, and her salvation like a torch that is burning. The nations will see your righteousness, and all kings your glory; and you will be called by a new name which the mouth of the Lord will designate.
>
> Behold, the Lord has proclaimed to the end of the earth, say to the daughter of Zion, "Lo, your salvation comes; behold His reward is with Him, and His recompense before Him." And they will call them, the holy people, the redeemed of the Lord; and you will be called, "Sought out, a city not forsaken." (Isa. 62:1–2, 11–12)

This is a prophetic picture of spiritual Israel under the leadership of the Messiah (Christ). While it is true that the gospel of Christ did "go forth" from the literal city of Jerusalem, *this* "Jerusalem" of prophecy is talking about God's people, His church, not Judea's city (Heb. 12:22; see also Rev 3:12, 21:1–2). The church will stand on the mountain of Christ's integrity, worthiness, and divine authority; it will worship on that "mountain" as a singular people who identify with the Savior and obey His voice. We see exactly this picture in *Revelation*:

> Then I looked, and behold, the Lamb was standing on Mount Zion, and with Him one hundred and forty-four thousand, having His name and the name of His Father written on their foreheads. And I heard a voice from heaven, like the sound of many waters and like the sound of loud thunder, and the voice which I heard was like the sound of harpists playing on their harps. And they sang a new song before the throne and before the four living creatures and the elders; and no one could learn the song except the one hundred and forty-four thousand who had been purchased from the earth. (Rev. 14:1–3)

This "one hundred and forty-four thousand" is not a literal number but a symbolic one. It represents the church *on the earth* that stands with Christ on His mountain, the bedrock of His authority as the King of God's kingdom. The two things—mountain and city, or Zion and Jerusalem—are inextricably related but not interchangeable. Despite Rome having declared war against Christ's church, John sees (and hears) the church standing safely and securely on Zion with the Lord Himself—a grand and triumphant scene!

Summary Thoughts: For His own reasons, God allowed a four-nation kingdom of men to dominate the world for centuries before finally bringing it to an end. The cause of its ending was the presentation of God's kingdom to the world through the reign of His Son as its King.

"Zion" and "Jerusalem" in messianic prophecies refer to Christ's authority and His church, respectively. His church had to be built upon His kingly authority; it could not be built until He had proven Himself worthy to be its head and had received His Father's kingdom. Once He sat down at the right hand of God—in essence, establishing "Zion"—He built His church, which rested upon His enthronement. "Zion" symbolizes His authority and reign; "Jerusalem" symbolizes the community of God's people who assemble to worship God in spirit and truth *by* that authority and reign.

One thing this study should reveal is the consistency between OT messianic prophecies and NT realities. What God promised, Christ fulfilled; the symbolism (and shadows) revealed through the ancient prophets are realized (made substantive) by Christ. Thus, "He is before all things, and in Him all things hold together" (Col. 1:17)—things of the material world, the spiritual world, and the salvation of human souls. Christ is not part of God's plan for our salvation; He *is* the plan.

From here we will begin looking at the spiritual influence and impact that the kingdom of God has upon the world, both through its citizens and whatever else Christ does in the human realm.

Chapter Nine

The Present and Future Kingdom

"When Jesus had finished these words, the crowds were amazed at His teaching; for He was teaching them as one having authority, and not as their scribes" (Mat. 7:28–29). Jesus had just delivered the most important sermon the world had ever heard. In doing so, He turned the Jews' world on its head, revealing the spiritual significance of a law they had only viewed as a legal document with technical language.

Jesus also foreshadowed what was coming, and now is, regarding the coming kingdom and what is expected of its citizens. To anyone who was paying attention, He did not have to literally introduce Himself as the King of Israel. His miracles underscored the heavenly origin of His message, and His message was all about God's kingdom and His Son's kingship. It was obvious that, in the words of Nicodemus, "no one can do these signs that You do unless God is with Him" (John 3:2). "If by God's power Jesus was casting out evil spirits, said Christ [Mat. 12:28], then the reign of God was being publicly revealed. The reign of God was being exhibited right before their eyes."[71]

The Age that Was Coming (and Now Is): The so-called sermon on the mount (Mat. 5 – 7) was the core message of the kingdom of God. This was a new message introducing a new age. The age of the world of darkness had taken its toll upon God's people. It had blinded their eyes, impeded their hearing, dulled their senses, and prevented many of them from receiving the message of the kingdom (Mat. 13:15–17). The age of the darkness had deluded God's people to think that they could earn righteousness through personal merit, good works, and keeping religious laws.

Then came the Light of the world, a Man unlike any man the Jews or the world had ever seen. He was a Man of Light bringing a message of enlightenment to a world shrouded in moral and religious darkness. "The Light shines in the darkness, and the darkness did not comprehend it" (John 1:5). The people of darkness did not "comprehend" or grasp the meaning of the Light that walked in their midst.

The world of darkness does not merely coexist with the age of the kingdom of God. It is set against it in defiance and hostility. Likewise, those who identify with the world of darkness are also hostile to Christ and "cannot please God" (Rom. 8:6–8). Those who follow "the flesh" (i.e., the carnal, satanic spirit born of human pride) and those who follow the Spirit of the kingdom "are in opposition to one another" (Gal. 5:16–17). There is no spiritual compatibility between these two worlds, two ages, and two kingdoms. The kingdom of darkness is an enemy of the kingdom of Light, and the kingdom of Light is gradually destroying the kingdom of darkness.

The Jews may have understood all this, except that they believed the kingdom of God would usher in the end of the world of darkness and bring into existence the world of Light, with no coexistence.[72] The idea of two worlds—two kingdoms—existing at once was difficult for the Jews to imagine, having been led to believe that the one would replace the other. But we see it today: God's spiritual kingdom exists, and the physical, sin-filled kingdom of wickedness also exists. These are incompatible kingdoms, enemies of each other, yet both exist at the same time. However, this will not always be the case: in the age to come—the afterlife—there will only be one kingdom, and all rival kingdoms will be destroyed.

> The New Testament sets The Age to Come [the kingdom of God] in direct opposition to This Age [the kingdom of darkness]. The present age is evil, but the Kingdom of God belongs to The Age to Come. The Kingdom of God, both as the perfect manifestation of God's reign and the realm of completed redemptive blessing, belongs to The Age to Come.[73]

> Thus we find that the Kingdom of God belongs to The Age to Come and is set in sharp contrast to This Age. In This Age there

is death; in the Kingdom of God, eternal life. In This Age, the righteous and the wicked are mixed together; in the Kingdom of God, all wickedness and sin will be destroyed. For the present, Satan is viewed as the "god of this age"; but in The Age to Come, God's Kingdom, God's rule will have destroyed Satan, and righteousness will displace all evil.[74]

The four-empire statue which Nebuchadnezzar saw in his dream historically realized and spiritually symbolized the old world order (Dan. 2). This old order sought power, control, domination, and riches. It was rooted in human power, earthly territory, material wealth, and human slavery. It was an order or system that indulged in the carnal appetites of men, exploiting the weaknesses and helplessness of their fellow human beings, without mercy or compassion. It was an order that seemed powerful and unstoppable (for a time) but was rotten at its core, its foundation resting upon an incohesive mixture of iron and clay—a foundation that, despite the strength and glory of all that rested upon it, was doomed to fail.

The new world order—the kingdom of God, as revealed through Christ and His enthronement—does not rely at all upon human power, material wealth, or earthly territory. It does not seek to exploit people but to enrich them with spiritual blessings. It does not enslave people to yet another form of human oppression, securing a disproportionate amassing of wealth and power for a very few at the expense of everyone else. Rather, it unburdens them from the greatest burden that has ever plagued humankind: sin.

The kingdom of God does have a King, but He is a kind, benevolent, and charitable King. He seeks the best interest of His citizens, which also serves the best interest of His kingdom. As God had prophesied about Him:

> Behold, My Servant, whom I uphold; My chosen one in whom My soul delights. I have put My Spirit upon Him; He will bring forth justice to the nations. He will not cry out or raise His

voice, nor make His voice heard in the street. A bruised reed He will not break and a dimly burning wick He will not extinguish; He will faithfully bring forth justice. (Isa. 42:1–3)

The world had never seen a king like this—one that spoke for the underprivileged and sought perfect, unbiased, and incorruptible justice. The world was familiar with cruel dictators, despots, tyrannical rulers who cared little or nothing for the welfare of their people. At best, it might have enjoyed a king that meant well but was politically weak, morally flawed, or simply a well-intentioned but inept ruler. History is littered with all these kinds of men, from one extreme to the other. Even in the record of the kings of Israel we see despots (Ahab) and useless kings (Baasha) and everything in-between.

But this glorious King to whom God the Father entrusted His own kingdom is transcendent in every respect. His character is flawless; His virtues, divine. He rules with perfect wisdom, infallible ability, and uncorrupted love. He does not reign from a place on earth but sits at the right hand of God Himself, and He is the One to which all Creation owes its existence. He is "the way, and the truth, and the life" (John 14:6), and He oversees all that has come into being with love, light, and truth.

The King's kindness and benevolence do not make Him unable to exercise judgment against those who oppose Him, however. "For not even the Father judges anyone, but He has given all judgment to the Son, so that all will honor the Son even as they honor the Father. He who does not honor the Son does not honor the Father who sent Him" (John 5:22–23). Those who refuse to honor the King (Son of God) will face His wrath and be destroyed (as depicted in Luke 19:27 and symbolically portrayed in Rev. 19:11–21). He has the right and power to enforce God's laws and punish those who defy them.

But Christ did not receive God's kingdom to destroy but to save. Salvation through redemption is His highest objective; He does not seek earthly wealth, earthly territory, or earthly power but the rescue of human souls from the oppression of sin and moral darkness. He does not want this objective to be blurred by or lost in church religion or human ministries that masquerade as being well-intentioned but are self-serving in nature. He does not want His citizens to forget why they *became* citizens in the first place—not to pursue a lifetime of worship services and church protocol but to represent the heavenly King to souls in desperate need of His leadership.

The power of God's kingdom, under Christ's leadership, has come into our world, bringing with it love, light, and truth. Those who set their minds on the Holy Spirit of this kingdom are filled with "life and peace" (Rom. 8:6). They are taught to love like God loves, walk in light as God is Light, and live by the truth that God has revealed to them in His word. These people are not merely religious, spiritual-minded, or churchgoers; they are genuine citizens of a kingdom that is not of this world. They also look forward to a reward that is far beyond this world. They are not church seekers but truth seekers, and God's truth always leads people to His kingdom.

Your Kingdom Came: In what has been traditionally called "the Lord's Prayer" (Mat. 6:9–13), Jesus taught His disciples to pray, "Your kingdom come" (6:10). Jesus had been preaching, "The kingdom of God is at hand" (Mat. 4:17), as did John the Baptist (Mat. 3:2). What Jesus taught His disciples is consistent with this: the kingdom had not yet been given over to the Son—His work on earth in preparation for this was, at this time, unfinished. He had yet to preach about the kingdom to the cities of Israel, proving His authority with many miracles. He had yet to die a sacrificial death, be buried, and then be resurrected from the grave. He had yet to spend forty days with His disciples and then ascend to heaven in their presence (Acts 1:1–11). Only then, after these things had been accomplished, did He in fact receive the kingdom from His Father.

But now that these things *have* all been accomplished, God's kingdom *has* been revealed to the world, and through the power and authority of this kingdom His will *is* accomplished on earth as it is in heaven. God's kingdom *has* come: it has "come" in the revelation of Christ as its King and all that He accomplishes in this supreme role. "The kingdom of God is that moral and spiritual kingdom which the God of grace is setting up in this fallen world, whose subjects consist of as many as have been brought into hearty subjection to His gracious scepter, and of which His Son Jesus is the glorious Head."[75]

To continue to pray, "Your kingdom come," ignores or does not understand what has happened. Christ is not going to be King; He is one now. God's kingdom is not going to come to us; it is already here. Praying this line ("Your kingdom come") may also manifest a misunderstanding of what "kingdom" means here.

Some want to see God's kingdom as continually "coming" into the lives of those who hear of and believe in it. While this view may have some merit, it is inconsistent with the context of Jesus' words and His preaching. Jesus' message was that the kingdom of God was ready to be revealed to the world. "But an hour is coming, and now is, when the true worshipers will worship the Father in spirit and truth; for such people the Father seeks to be His worshipers" (John 4:23). This "coming, and now is" accurately depicts the situation as Jesus meant it in Mat. 6:10: the kingdom *is* coming, and is so close and anticipated, it is as if it is *now* here.

The Future of the Kingdom: In a unique passage, Paul says that Christ must reign as King until He "hands over the kingdom to the God and Father, when He has abolished all rule and all authority and power. For He must reign until He has put all His enemies under His feet" (1 Cor. 15:24–25). Paul calls this "the end," which begs the question: the "end" of what? He answers this in part by claiming that God will put all Christ's enemies "under His feet." This alludes to an ancient practice of a victorious king or military leader putting his foot on the neck of the defeated kings (as in Josh. 10:24). It is a visible demonstration of the full authority of the victor and the complete subjugation of the vanquished.

All rival kingdoms, principalities, and authorities must be "abolished." This does not mean that Christ is presently fighting for supremacy over all such kingdoms; His Father's kingdom is already (and has always been) in supreme command over all that has been created. What it *does* mean is that all rival kingdoms will acknowledge this supremacy and will, in the process, be forced to unconditionally surrender all their power. In the end, there will only be one kingdom that exists, and Christ's church will be a part of that kingdom forever. "This divine kingdom goes back to the beginning and rules the world and shall rule until the consummation at the end of time. All that is in the world, even every hostile force, is subservient to the plans of God."[76]

But "the end" does not only concern what happens to Christ's enemies. It also implies the end (completion) of why Christ was made King over the Father's kingdom in the first place. As discussed earlier, the purpose of His reign is for the redemption of human souls. Once the opportunity for this redemption has run its full course and the physical universe has been brought to a fiery end (2 Peter 3:10–12), there will be no more need or opportunity for redemption. All the redeemed (Christ's church) will be ushered into glory. All those who refused or forfeited this redemption will be cast into outer darkness (Rev. 21:7–8). There will be no more preaching the gospel, converting souls to Christ, or carrying out the work of God amid a sinful world. The world, both literally and figuratively, will be gone; the ransomed will be forever with God. This is what He has always wanted; this is the "eternal purpose" of creating human beings in the first place (Eph. 3:11–12).

To hand the kingdom back to the Father does not mean that Christ will be demoted. It is, in the context of Paul's words, an expression of accomplishment: what both the Father and His Son set out to do, they did. There is nothing more to do in the context of redemption and salvation; the King's work will be completely fulfilled. From that point forward, there will be no need for Christ to function in His role as King and High Priest any longer.

Paul is not talking about a mere end of an era; he is also talking about the beginning of an eternal communion with the Father, His Son, and

His Spirit. Maybe a parallel idea would be that of a sitting United States President who has fulfilled his term in office. He steps aside, not because of demotion but because the purpose for which he was elected has been fulfilled. In fact, he may still be referred to as "Mr. President" even after he leaves office, because he will forever be remembered for the service he rendered to his country.

Will there be a kingdom in the eternity to come? Of course. God has always had a kingdom, and He will always have a kingdom. He is still "a great King" (Mal. 1:14) and will never cease to be this. In the glorious future, all the redeemed will forever be citizens of this kingdom.[77] They will not worship the King in faith, as we do now, but in fact. They will "see the King in His beauty" (Isa. 33:17); they will bow before His visible presence; they will speak with Him face to face.

In that future context, there will be no need for faith, hope, prayer, mercy, grace, or forgiveness. These are all a part of the present kingdom; these are all necessary for redemption. In the future kingdom, no one will need forgiveness because sin and temptation will no longer plague God's people. There will be no covenant relationship because the ransomed will already be in a relationship with God that will never be corrupted or come to an end. The only reason for God to make covenants with people is to reconcile them to Himself through faith and grace (rather than law and justice). In a world where there is no sin, there is also no need to deal with it.[78]

The Myth of a Thousand-year Reign: I said earlier that many people have a misunderstanding of what the Bible teaches concerning the kingdom of God. One common misunderstanding is to view the kingdom as a future one-thousand-year reign of Christ, also known as millennialism. According to this modern doctrine, this is the basic sequence of events:

- Christ will "rapture" all faithful Christians—literally, the entire church—from the earth and bring them into heaven with Him. This will leave the world without any Christians (or children, some say), only the Bible.

- A satanic global leader (or a ten-nation confederacy, some say) will take over and make Christianity illegal throughout the world, among other fiats of power and domination. (He is often dubbed "the Antichrist," "the Beast," or both.) This situation will continue for three-and-a-half years, during which time all who become Christians will be hated but still legally tolerated.
- In the next three-and-a-half years, however, the Antichrist will launch a global and murderous persecution of all those who since have become Christians. These two three-and-a-half year periods comprise what is known as a seven-year Tribulation.
- At the end of the seven-year Tribulation will be a cataclysmic war between the Antichrist (in which two hundred million men will fight) and Christ's army of angels—a battle known as Armageddon (citing Rev. 16:13–16).
- Christ will decisively win this battle and will cast the Antichrist and his accomplices into the "lake of fire," and Satan will be "bound" with a "great chain" for "a thousand years" (Rev. 20:1–3).
- It is at this point that, allegedly, the temple of God will be rebuilt in Jerusalem and Christ will reign there in the flesh for a thousand years. Not only this, but 144,000 Jews will be "sealed" by God to serve Christ as glorified emissaries throughout the world. (There are numerous variations of this account.) *This*, it is said, is the kingdom that Christ wanted all along—an earthly, millennial, and Jerusalem-based kingdom. The Jews—the people who rejected Christ as their King and had Him executed on a cross, bringing upon themselves an awful curse (Luke 19:41–44)—will then, inexplicably, have preferential treatment in this new, earthly, and millennial kingdom.

It goes beyond the intent of this study to disprove all the points of this modern doctrine, since we are seeking what the Bible teaches the kingdom *is*, not what people *think* it is. On the other hand, since this doctrine is so widely believed as "the truth," a limited response is in order.

First, *Revelation* is, from Rev. 4:1 to 22:6, John's account of a vision given to him by Christ. The entire book was written to "the seven churches of

Asia," which Christ identifies in 1:10–11. It does not describe the great conflict that will occur in *our* future, but what will occur ("soon") in *their* lifetime and shortly beyond.

The visionary context cannot be arbitrarily interpreted as literal and symbolic. The context is *all* symbolic, unless John (the writer) says otherwise. Thus, "one thousand years"—and all other numbers, time frames, and measurements—are symbolic, not literal.

The only place where John mentions Christ and "thousand years" together is in Rev. 20:4. The context, again, is symbolic, not literal; John says nothing about *where* this reign occurs, only that it does. It never says anywhere in the NT that Christ did, will, wanted to, or even needed to reign for a thousand years in a newly built temple in Jerusalem.

For all the trouble that the apostle Paul went through to show that there is no distinction between Jews and Gentiles "in Christ Jesus" (Gal. 3:28), to say that God will reinstate such a distinction in the end-times contradicts all NT Scripture. God's relationship with the Jews *as a national or ethnic people* has long since been over; He proved this when He had the Romans level Jerusalem to the ground in AD 70. His salvation is open to *all* people, both Jews and Gentiles, just as His judgment will be rendered to *all* people, regardless of ethnicity; "For there is no partiality with God" (Rom. 2:5–11).

There is no purpose for Christ to reign on earth for a thousand years. It proves nothing more than what has already been proven; to maintain otherwise denies what He *has* done. He prayed, "I glorified You on the earth, having accomplished the work which You have given Me to do. Now, Father, glorify Me together with Yourself, with the glory which I had with You before the world was" (John 17:4–5). He was done here; He *is* done here. He has no intention of returning here and no reason to do so.

Rather than a "first rapture" (as it is sometimes called) of all the Christians from the earth, while allowing the rest of the world continue as it was, there will be a resurrection of the dead "in Christ," and then Christians "who are alive [i.e., still living] and remain will be caught up together" with the resurrected believers" (see 1 Thess. 4:13–18). Call this being "caught up" a rapture if you want to (the Latin translation here is *rapio*, from which we get "rapture"), but this event marks the end of time, not the beginning of a seven-year Tribulation. After this, Christ will unleash a fiery judgment against "those who do not know God and to those who do not obey the gospel of our Lord Jesus" (2 Thess. 1:6–10).

There is nothing said in the NT, outside of the visionary and purposely symbolic context of *Revelation*, of a partial rapture, seven-year Tribulation, or a literal battle of Armageddon. There is nothing said of a literal binding of Satan (the "chain," we are told is symbolic, but the "thousand years" is literal—all arbitrarily determined, in the same verse!), Christ's thousand-year reign in Jerusalem in a new temple, or Jews commissioned and sealed to represent Christ during that millennium. These are, among many elements of millennialism, plucked out of thin air, forced into the Scriptures, taught as divine truth, and received by those who have been indoctrinated with this teaching.

The implications of millennialism, too, are unacceptable. This doctrine implies, among other untenable teachings:

- Christ really did *not* finish all "the work" which the Father sent Him to earth to do, despite what Christ said (John 17:4–5).
- Christ *failed* to do all this work. This forces the kingdom of God to be limited to heaven; the church is the only evidence of His kingdom on the earth.
- Even though Christ failed in His first attempt to (allegedly) establish an earthly kingdom, and even though He said He never had any intention of doing this (see John 6:15 and 18:36–37), we are told that *next time*—in the thousand-year reign—He will succeed. But if He failed the first time—in any way, for any reason—why should we believe He will succeed the second time? And what would any failure say of His worthiness to be our King?

- God has lingering, unfinished, and covenantal obligations toward the nation of Israel (Jews) that have yet to be honored, and (allegedly) will be honored in Christ's thousand-year reign. This idea undermines the fact that Christ has fulfilled God's covenant with Israel and that it is still in effect. It also paints God as a sometimes-dishonorable God.
- God, despite being impartial toward all people regarding salvation, will become partial toward the Jews and give them preferential treatment (because of the point above). This creates a different means of salvation than one predicated on human faith (see Rom. 5:1–2), since Jesus is not Someone who one must believe exists because of the recorded evidence but can be seen with one's own eyes, not his heart.
- Despite *Revelation* having been written to the seven churches of the Roman province of Asia, many have turned it instead to a fanciful depiction of what will happen in our future. This ignores the historical, contextual, and biblical context of *Revelation* and the rest of the NT. Much, much more could be said on this.

That is the short list. The long list is, well, considerably lengthy and detailed. Regardless, the modern "take" on the kingdom of God is far more rooted in starry-eyed end-of-the-world expectations rather than serious attempts to study it (and related subjects) biblically. Much of the religious world has made up its mind concerning the kingdom, having made their church dogma dependent upon these conclusions. Changing their view of the kingdom would detrimentally affect other beliefs as well—and they may not be willing to do this.

Summary Thoughts: Jesus came into the human realm as "the Light of the world" (John 8:12). No one had ever seen such Light before; no one could have ever predicted how truly amazing He was. His words pierced the darkness and penetrated the people's hearts. He spoke with authority, confidence, and conviction; "Never has a man spoken the way this man speaks" (John 7:46). His miracles—numerous, diverse, and unpredictable—proved beyond a shadow of doubt that He came from God and was Himself a divine Being.

His purpose, however, was not merely to speak and perform miracles. These things were all part of a bigger picture: to bring the kingdom of God into the world of human beings. This kingdom would manifest itself in the work of God's Spirit, the gospel message, the conversion of souls and transformation of sinners' lives, and the overtaking of the domain of darkness with the kingdom of Light.

The age of the world is being overtaken by the age of the Kingdom: one will prevail over the other, endure beyond the other, and destroy the other. For now, both kingdoms coexist but are not at all in league with each other. They are instead great enemies, and those who give allegiance to one are opposed to those who give allegiance to the other. Christians, as citizens of the kingdom of God, are not to have any spiritual fellowship with those who are not citizens. Christians belong to Christ's church (as a community of believers) but only because each Christian has first made Christ as Lord (King) in his heart.

"The future has invaded the present. ... Tomorrow has met today. The Age to Come has entered This Age. The life of tomorrow is offered to us in the here and now."[79] The age of the Kingdom will continue into the eternity to come. There is no one on the planet who cannot become a citizen of this kingdom now to enjoy the glory of the kingdom in the afterlife. The King is so powerful, He can overcome every sin, every obstacle, every circumstance, and every enemy.

Do you believe this?

Chapter Ten

A New World Order

"When Jesus saw the crowds, He went up on the mountain; and after He sat down, His disciples came to Him" (Mat. 5:1). Jesus introduced the kingdom of God to the nation of Israel as a new world order. And this is as it should be since it revolutionized everything the Israelites—and the world—understood about a kingdom.

Fifteen hundred years earlier, God had the people of Israel—as they were barely a nation yet—at the base of Mt Sinai in the wilderness. God had just led them out of Egypt where they had been enslaved for over four hundred years. They were told who this God was (the "I AM WHO I AM," "the God of your fathers" Abraham, Isaac, and Jacob—Exod. 3:14–15), but they had never been formally introduced.

This introduction was a terrifying experience for the people (Exod. 19:16–19). The mountain was shrouded in smoke, and lightning and thunder exploded from it. A "very loud trumpet sound" emanated from the mountain, bringing an awful dread to all who heard it. The earth quaked as well, and the Israelites "trembled and stood at a distance" from the base of the mountain, lest they be struck dead, as God promised would happen if they came too close.

Then God began speaking from the mountain in His own voice to the people. He spoke what we know as the Ten Commandments (Exod. 20:1–17), His voice thundering while the mountain continued to smoke. The people were so terrified that they wanted to run away and let Moses deal with God on his own. But Moses said, "Do not be afraid; for God has come in order to test you, and in order that the fear of Him may remain with you, so that you may not sin" (Exod. 19:19–20).

But who could *not* be afraid of this imposing scenario? Even Moses at some point in this event said, "I am full of fear and trembling"

(Heb. 12:21). This scene gave the people of Israel a taste of who it was they were dealing with—really, of who was dealing with *them*. God intentionally exhibited Himself with powerful signs and sounds that He knew would command respect.

Before He could move forward with this people, they had to know that He was an all-powerful God, a far greater force than anything they had experienced from the Egyptians. Law and order needed to be established up front with an indelible memory of who God is.

Fast-forward fifteen hundred years, and we see Jesus sitting quietly and approachably upon a hill somewhere in Galilee. It is probably a peaceful, sunny day. "He opened His mouth and began to teach them" (Mat. 5:2), but not in a thunderous voice. It is the calm yet authoritative voice of a prophet—of *the* Prophet, the One who was greater than all the prophets combined. This is the Son of God, and He has come to visit His people.

A New Beginning: In one sense, nothing had changed. The Jews came out of their homes, away from their jobs, and away from all that they had become accustomed to. John the Baptist, a kind of Moses figure, had been preparing the people for this meeting for the previous six months. Just as the Israelites at Mt Sinai had to prepare themselves to meet God (Exod. 19:9–11), many Jews had been baptized by John, confessing and repenting of their sins, and ready to hear the words of the Prophet. God the Son presented Himself on a mountain with a message for His people—a message that, like the Ten Commandments, would introduce a new era and a new relationship between God and men.

Yet, in another sense, everything had changed. Being in Jesus' presence was not terrifying but quiet, intriguing, even exciting. There was no smoke, lightning, thunder, or earthquake. Jesus' disciples approached Him without fear, and especially without fear of being killed if they came too close. No one wanted to run away; if anything, His calm but authoritative and commanding voice brought assurance and stability to the situation. He was not unsure of Himself; He did not defer to rabbinic teachers nearly twice His age; He did not hesitate, stumble over His words, or ever apologize for anything He said. He knew who He was, from whence He came, and the profound importance of His mission.

Jesus was not just delivering a sermon on that mountain. He was upending an entire system of religion that had become so entrenched with human ideas, human misunderstanding, and human corruption that it had to be replaced with something better. The covenant God made with Israel on Mt Sinai fifteen hundred years before needed to be fulfilled—not terminated, but fulfilled, as in kept perfectly—so that a new covenant could be made. The old covenant was becoming obsolete; the new covenant ushered in new things, better things (Heb. 8:6, 13), and a superior teaching that would revolutionize the world.

Jesus came to fulfill that original covenant. He did not come to change the Law of Moses (Mat. 5:17–19) but to bring it to completion, to give it appropriate closure. In anticipation of this new covenant, Jesus began talking about the kind of person—really, the kind of *heart*—that could participate in the new world order and the kind of people that it would produce. He invited the Jews to ascend with Him to another level of fellowship with God unlike what they had become accustomed to. He invited them to see God in a new light, not as a terrifying God that would destroy all who came near Him. Rather, He invited them to come near to God *through Him*, the King.

The new world order is not a mere new religion. This perspective is a mistaken one, sometimes unconsciously promoted (in the way we may speak of "Christianity," for example). Rather, this new order concerns Christ's rescue of those who wish to "escape from the snare of the devil, having been held captive by him to do his will" (2 Tim. 2:26). It is, in Christ's own words, "to open their eyes so that they may turn from darkness to light and from the dominion of Satan to God, that they may receive forgiveness of sins and an inheritance among those who have been sanctified by faith in Me" (Acts 26:18).

Christ's kingdom is not only a new order for those who submit to Him (Christians). It is a new order for the entire world. His influence as the

King of kings and Lord of lords permeates all human history in every place where His gospel is known. While every nation has its ruler(s) and all people are subject to some form of human authority, the world knows—intuitively, if not specifically—that there is a *higher authority* which every person must answer to in the life to come. Apart from such an authority, it is impossible for people to be held morally responsible for their actions and receive either a reward or punishment based on this.[80]

A King not only exists but is necessary. This King must be all-knowing and all-powerful, else He cannot serve as the Judge of all humankind. In other words, He must know all things about all people accurately, impartially, and absolutely. He must know what it means to be human, having personally experienced the human condition (with all its trials, temptations, and sufferings). The new world order begins with the introduction of this King:

> Therefore having overlooked the times of ignorance, God is now declaring to men that all people everywhere should repent, because He has fixed a day in which He will judge the world in righteousness through a Man whom He has appointed, having furnished proof to all men by raising Him from the dead. (Acts 17:30–31)

The phrase "all people everywhere" and "all men" is universal in scope. The King—"Jesus Christ the righteous" (1 John 2:1)—is not merely an authority to Christians but to the entire human race. Christians have given their allegiance to the King, but His kingship oversees "all people everywhere." Christians may acknowledge His kingdom more accurately than everyone else, but this kingdom both transcends and rules over all other kingdoms, in the physical realm as well as the spiritual. No one can excuse himself from the King's oversight; no one can claim exemption from His kingdom; no one has so-called diplomatic immunity that protects him from the King's authority.

A World Turned Right-side-up: Jesus defined the kingdom of God in ways that contradict the old order (or, the old Creation). Throughout history, there have been established expectations that all people understood were seemingly normal, though not always pleasant. (I am thinking of the words, "some things will never change," from Bruce Hornsby's 1986 song, "That's Just the Way It Is.")

For example, we expect: first come, first served; wealth is power; might makes right; those with all the gold make all the rules; earthly status is important; etc. We expect powerful people to deserve the most attention. We expect rulers to lord themselves over their people. We idolize celebrities and lightly regard humble people. We idolize youthful beauty and dismiss the elderly with silver hair and wrinkled skin. We idolize sex and do not value godly love. We see servitude as a form of weakness and lowliness as a form of insecurity.

This is just what we (people) do as a matter of habit. The kingdoms of men, so to speak, abide by the natural course and expectation of human behavior. Human nature, and expectations based upon human nature, will always remain essentially unchanged.

Humans do not rule over the kingdom of God, however, but the Son of God does. Human souls are part of the kingdom but do not dictate its objectives, principles, or behaviors. God's kingdom operates by a heavenly standard which is far above all earthly ones. Its expectations are not equal to those of worldly people; its values far transcend those of people who are not influenced by its King.

We are tempted to think that the kingdom of God is upside-down from the world, yet the truth is that the world has been upside-down since the Fall (i.e., Adam and Eve's disobedience in the Garden). Sin has corrupted not only our souls but our thinking, our perspective, and our dealings with others. The sinful world has convinced us that it is strong while belief in God is weak, that it has science and answers while God has only myths and fairy tales, and that billions of people cannot be wrong about all their unchristian religious beliefs.

Yet the kingdom of God is right-side-up—it has always been and always will be this way. The world operates in a shroud of lies, deceptions, and wickedness; it is blind to its true nature. The kingdom has exposed the world for what it really is: a massive, sinful, and hopeless fraud. Paul warned us that "the god of this world has blinded the minds of the unbelieving so that they might not see the light of the gospel of the glory of Christ, who is the image of God" (2 Cor. 4:4). In other words, the godless world convinces people that they can see when in fact they are blind to what is really happening to them. "[I]f a blind man guides a blind man, both will fall into a pit" (Mat. 15:14).

The kingdom is all about love, light, and truth; the satanic world is all about apathy, perversity, and deception. In Mat. 11:1–6, John the Baptist sent some of his disciples to ask if Jesus was "the Expected One, or shall we look for someone else?" Jesus pointed to His miracles as proof of the answer: only God's Messiah could do these things by His own authority. Then He said, "And blessed is he who does not take offense at Me." We cannot be offended when the kingdom of God does not meet our expectations. And we must see it in the context of the spiritual battle that Jesus waged against the domain of darkness. What Jesus meant, then, was this:

> Yes, the Kingdom of God is here. But there is a mystery—a new revelation about the Kingdom. The Kingdom of God is here; but instead of destroying human sovereignty, it has attacked the sovereignty of Satan. The Kingdom of God is here; but instead of making changes in the external, political order of things, it is making changes in the spiritual order and in the lives of men and women.[81]

This is a critically important perspective. The kingdom's purpose is not to bring about church services, social change, or governmental reform. It is to fight "against the world forces of this darkness, against the spiritual forces of wickedness in the heavenly places" (Eph. 6:12). This fight is conducted not only in the world generally but in each believer individually.[82]

God's word teaches citizens of His kingdom to rise above the world's darkness and wickedness, to attain to a higher and nobler kind of thinking than the world can reach on its own. "Therefore, having these promises [of God, to be called His sons and daughters—see 2 Cor. 6:17–18], beloved, let us cleanse ourselves from all defilement of flesh and spirit, perfecting holiness in the fear of God" (2 Cor. 7:1, bracketed words added). This is not church language but kingdom language. We do not perfect holiness on our own but we most certainly participate in the process. We denounce the self-serving character of this world; we choose instead to be "conformed to the image of [God's] Son" in response to His having called us through His gospel (Rom. 8:29; see 2 Thess. 2:13–14).

Things are not always what they seem in the kingdom of God. We cannot assess it by human standards because it transcends these (1 Cor. 2:12–16, in principle). Accordingly, Jesus made sharp contrasts between the world's expectations and those of His kingdom:

- "Blessed are you when people insult you and persecute you, and falsely say all kinds of evil against you because of Me" (Mat. 5:11). This seems backward or upside-down, but in God's world, suffering for what is right is highly commendable (1 Peter 3:13–14). The world condemns what it does not understand, what exposes its faults, or what interferes with its agenda. Christ praises those who will stand up for truth and righteousness, just as He did—even to His own hurt. Sometimes a believer will be like a soldier in a foxhole, holding his position despite bullets flying overhead and bombs exploding nearby. Still, he has something to defend, and faith in his cause and courage under fire keep him focused on his mission.
- "Beware of practicing your righteousness before men to be noticed by them; otherwise you have no reward with your Father who is in heaven" (Mat. 6:1). The world, and worldly-minded religious people, want to be recognized for their expressions of piety, gestures of charity, and other good deeds (see Luke 18:9–17). In the kingdom of God, it is only necessary that the King see these things; it is unnecessary and even shameful to call attention to them for the

purpose of human praise.

- Heavenly treasure is more real and satisfying than earthly treasure (Mat. 6:19–21). The world either does not believe in spiritual treasure or does not value it. God's world is not about what is seen and temporary but what is unseen and eternal (2 Cor. 4:16–18). The world thinks it foolish to forego earthly wealth (and fame, power, popularity, etc.) for the sake of an unseen and otherworldly reward; Jesus says it is foolish to ignore the needs of one's eternal soul for the things of this world (Mat. 16:26).
- "the last shall be first, and the first last" (see Mat. 20:1–16 for the full context). This turns the world's perspective on its head: it does not seem fair to the world and therefore is rejected. But the world's system of fairness is based upon self-interest, or on a personal view of justice. God's system is based upon what serves the best interest of all parties.
- Greatness in God's kingdom is based on servitude, not "lording" oneself over others or exalting oneself at another's expense (Mat. 20:26–28). Servitude, in the world's eyes, often seems weak, degrading, and unprofitable; in God's kingdom, servitude is the route to true greatness, and He will highly exalt those who humble their hearts to Him and serve people (1 Peter 5:5–6).
- Those who claim to "see" (by their own human, finite, and corrupted view of themselves) are blind, and those who acknowledge their blindness (by the illumination of God's word) can see (John 9:39–41). The kingdom of God does not blind people to their sinful nature, but the world does. The kingdom enlightens the human soul with divine truth, which is at odds with the so-called "truth" of human understanding (compare John 3:18–21).
- The world seeks "the approval of men *rather than* the approval of God" (John 12:42–43, emphasis added). The world seeks human praise, approval, and commendation; the kingdom of God values only the King's praise and approval (2 Cor. 10:18). Jesus said to the money- and power-loving Pharisees, "You are those who justify yourselves in the sight of men, but God knows your hearts; for that which is highly esteemed among men is detestable in the sight of God" (Luke 16:15). Sadly, this observation has broad application.

Other contrasts exist, but the point is clear. The concerns, priorities, and values of God's kingdom are superior in every respect to the flawed, inferior, and short-sighted agenda of the world. If everyone lived by the world's standards, with no influence from the King and His kingdom, the world would very quickly become like it was in the days of Noah, where "the wickedness of man was great on the earth, and that every intent of the thoughts of his heart was only evil continually" (Gen. 6:5). This would be a world not worth saving, a world so corrupted that God could do nothing but destroy it.

Yet if everyone in the world lived by the kingdom of God's standards, it would produce as close to a heavenly existence as could be imagined. Humankind would not be operating by an upside-down standard where everything is distorted, perverted, and self-serving. Rather, it would be an enlightened world in which everyone practiced love, light, and truth. People would not be competitive for self-preservation; everyone would be looking out for the best interest of his fellow man. Love would be the law of the land; every heart would be filled with the Light of the world; and truth would be a global language, uniting all people into a genuine brotherhood of kingdom citizens.

Again, it is the visible world that is upside-down, and it is the invisible kingdom of God that is right-side-up. Christians must never lose sight of this. God never follows people, but people who follow God are always improved.

Christians and the King: Christians are citizens of Christ's kingdom. However, we do not always speak of ourselves in this way. We tend to think of salvation in terms of conformity to required acts of obedience and membership in Christ's church. I do not want to imply that this is an altogether wrong kind of thinking (and I have written on these subjects extensively). Bringing a soul to Christ the Redeemer is exactly what we should do. Sinners need Christ's blood for atonement; a covenant relationship with God is the "place" (context) for that atonement; Christ's church is the sanctuary of those who are atoned. These things are right and good; they are biblical and truthful.

Yet it is possible that Christians fail to see the importance and relevance of Christ the King in our salvation. For example, when Peter says that we are to "sanctify Christ as Lord in your hearts," this lordship is not His relationship to His church but to the one who submits to His authority and rule as a great King. He is the head of His church, to be sure (Col. 1:18), but He must also be the head of your life. God made Him head of His church, but you must make Him Lord of your heart. He does not automatically become the Lord of anyone's heart only because He is the head of His church. A personal and necessary surrender of self-will is required to receive Him as your King.

As your King, Christ rules over you. This is a different context than your relationship with Him as the head of His church. That relationship governs the brotherhood and the doctrine that *defines* the brotherhood. His kingship governs your heart, affecting how you think, everything you do, and your relationships. Your heart and your life become His dominion. He oversees His church as a husband oversees his wife—with love, benevolence, and understanding. But He rules over one's heart as a great King, one who has royal authority to make decisions, command that you embrace divine truth and remove sinful practices, and pardon you when you have been atoned by His blood.

This is what it means to be a citizen of His kingdom: you make Him *your* King and you agree to submit to *His* authority. We should not confuse "kingdom life" with "church life," for while these are related, they are not the same thing. A person can "go to church" and even be active in its work and yet not be a citizen of God's kingdom. A person can conform to his congregation's expectations and yet not conform to the King's expectations. People can excel in church protocol while failing in kingdom righteousness.

We have become so used to talking, thinking, and behaving as "church" people that to speak of ourselves as citizens of God's kingdom may sound foreign, as if it is a new idea. To some, it may seem an open door to liberalism or heresy. Yet Jesus spoke often, openly, and passionately about the kingdom of God and was conspicuously silent (or nearly so) about the church. We, too, ought to speak often, openly, and passionately about His kingdom and kingdom living. Perhaps if we did so we would see the church in an entirely new light, not as a final objective but as a natural result of our alignment with God's kingdom.

The kingdom life is a blessed life; church life, if I can refer to it as such, is an outgrowth of that, not something separate. We should remember that God enthroned Christ as King before He made Him as head of His church. Likewise, we should recognize Christ's kingship over His kingdom as the means to understanding His headship over His church. Both contexts—kingdom and church, or kingship and headship—are important, and we do not want to pit one against the other or feel like we must choose one or the other. But we also do not want to blur the lines of distinction between the two out of convenience or any other reason. We do want to see the relevance of both as they affect our relationship with God and thus our salvation.

In time, Christ's church—the sanctuary of those who have submitted to Christ the King and are redeemed by the blood of Christ the High Priest—will be ushered into glory. The church will inherit the kingdom; the kingdom will not inherit the church. Christ's church will live forever as a glorious people who will no longer walk by faith but in fact dwell in the presence of the King.

At that time, the work of the kingdom of God under the leadership of His Son will have run its course; its objective will have been met; the new world order among humankind will be the eternal order for those ransomed from the world of flesh and blood. "For Jesus, the kingdom of God was the dynamic rule of God which had invaded history in His own person and mission to bring men in the present age the blessings of the messianic age, and which would manifest itself yet again at the end of the age to bring this messianic salvation to its consummation."[83]

Summary Thoughts: In His so-called sermon on the mount, Jesus did not merely offer a sermon to which people nod, smile with approval, and say "amen." Jesus was turning the religious world upside-down, the reverberating effects of which would turn the non-religious world upside-down as well.

Jesus did not come bringing more laws than what the Law of Moses had; He did not come as a successor to Moses or Elijah but as superior to both (a fact underscored in His transfiguration—Mat. 17:1–5). He did not come as a starry-eyed revolutionary, a social reformer, or a rebel against Rome. He was not seeking to reform the Law but to fulfill it; He was not offering the Jews an upgraded version of their present religion but an entirely new understanding of what it meant to walk with God.

Jesus came into the world to deal with sin—your sin, my sin, and every person on the planet's sin. He came not to destroy sinners but to destroy the sin *in* sinners, thus making them children of God. He came to reveal God the Father to us in a way no one else had the right or ability to do. He came to demonstrate God's love for us, His desire for our fellowship, and His reward for those who believe in His grace and forgiveness.

Jesus came into the world through a miracle (His virgin birth) and left the world miraculously (His resurrection and ascension). He did these things to show us that He came *from* God and has the power to bring us *to* God.

All people are subject to Christ's kingship in the sense that we all will answer to Him. But only Christians have voluntarily subjected themselves; everyone else is either insuperably ignorant (i.e., through circumstances beyond their control) of His kingship or is in some form of rebellion against Him. Morally-speaking, "the whole world lies in the power of the evil one" (1 John 5:19), but this does not mean that "the evil one" (Satan) has greater power than Christ the King. Even Satan will one day answer to Christ, and Christ will destroy Satan forever, not the other way around.

The kingdom of God does not pattern itself after the corrupted human world. Rather, the more people adopt the heart, message, and behavior of the kingdom, the better *their* world becomes. In God's world, as we perceive it, things are not always as they seem: the world thinks the kingdom of God is backward and upside-down when in fact it is the world that is backwardly and perversely oriented.

Christians would do well to pay more attention to kingdom living than churchgoing. This is not to diminish the need for churches, church attendance, and the work of individual churches. Rather, it is to emphasize the effect of the kingdom of God on the hearts of those involved in these things, to bring them to a higher level of thinking, understanding, and living.

This is where the King wants us: not merely singing about the kingdom in a church service but conforming to the King Himself and thus drawing ever nearer to His Father.

Part Three

Citizenship in the Kingdom

Chapter Eleven

The Blessedness of the Kingdom

> When Jesus saw the crowds, He went up on the mountain; and after He sat down, His disciples came to Him. He opened His mouth and began to teach them, saying … (Mat. 5:1–2)

We often refer to the first words Jesus said upon that mountain as the Beatitudes. This word is not in the original Greek text or anywhere in Scripture. It is a Latin word that is used to describe the kind of statements Jesus went on to make. (The original NT text was written in Koine Greek.) "Beatitude" means supreme happiness or blessedness, as a person who is blessed by God experiences.

When we say "happy" or "happiness," we may be tempted to think about what makes us happy in this life (family and friends, a vacation, a new car or home, a surplus of income, etc.). This is not what Jesus meant or ever intended to mean. Happiness, as God defines it, is contentment with Him. Paul expresses this best in Phil. 4:11–13: earthly circumstances come and go, change from better or worse, and may be enjoyed or lost, but contentment with God can remain constant. It is not dependent upon earthly status or circumstances; nor does it require optimal conditions for it to exist. It only requires that one's heart is in a right relationship with God—on His terms, not one's own.

These Beatitudes—statements of blessedness and spiritual contentment—run parallel in form to the Ten Commandments. These statements are essentially commandments: these things that Jesus said (be mournful, be merciful, be gentle, etc.) are not optional but required. They are not divine suggestions but divine expectations. However, they are not in a "Thus-says-the-Lord" formula, as what Israel heard from God at Sinai. Instead of emphasizing the commandment aspect of each statement, Jesus emphasizes the *consolation* or *reward* of keeping each of these expectations. God at Sinai emphasized law, authority, power, and punishment; Jesus on a hill in Galilee emphasized penitence, virtue, godliness, and reward.

We should not think, however, that Jesus words here (in Mat. 5:3–12) are at variance with the OT. These are not new ideas, but are timeless ones embedded in the Law and the Prophets. God has always taught His people to be humble, repentant, teachable, gentle, etc. To take this further, these are not statements about the church but the kingdom of God—and entrance into the kingdom is God's promise to the Jews.

Thus, Jesus did not direct these statements specifically at Christians (although they obviously apply to them) but to Jews who anticipated a glorious kingdom and their favored entrance into it. "[T]he language in which these Beatitudes are couched is purposely fetched from the Old Testament, to show that the new kingdom is but the old in a new form; while the characters described are but the varied forms of that spirituality which was the essence of real religion all along, but had well-nigh disappeared under corrupt teaching."[84]

Such words did, however, usher in a new beginning in people's relationship with God. From Mount Sinai, God spoke ten words (or commandments), "ten" symbolizing completeness in the context of human life.[85] Jesus spoke eight words (or statements), "eight" symbolizing a new beginning in Scripture—newness in time, power, status, and relationship with God.[86]

The Beatitudes: We benefit from examining these eight statements in the context in which Jesus meant them. Remember that "blessed" does not mean merely "happy" but content *with* God and *in* God. Note also that Jesus does not say, "Blessed *will be* thus-and-so" (future tense) but "Blessed *are*..." (present tense)—in other words, this is not a future expectation but is the real state of being of those who are citizens of the kingdom.

- ***"Blessed are the poor in spirit, for theirs is the kingdom of heaven"*** (Mat. 5:3). Jesus does not say, "Blessed are the poor," which gives special and unwarranted blessing to people only because of their economic destitution. The kingdom is not about economics, status, or ethnicity. It is about the condition of one's heart as it relates to the King and His kingdom. This is what Jesus means here—nothing more, but nothing less, either.
    - The "poor in spirit" are the humble-hearted. Their "poverty" does not concern their money but their pride, because human pride leads us to think we are rich and prosperous (apart from God) when in fact we are, as Jesus told the Laodiceans, "wretched and miserable and poor and blind and naked" (Rev. 3:17).
    - The "poor in spirit" humble themselves before God whereas before, in their arrogance, they had exalted themselves against God, leading them to sin against Him. Now they see their situation clearly—the Light of the kingdom has exposed them—and they come humbly before God seeking His favor. The kingdom of heaven welcomes such people with such hearts.[87]

- ***"Blessed are those who mourn, for they shall be comforted"*** (Mat. 5:4). Jesus does not say, "Blessed are all people who mourn" over circumstances they are in, losses they incur, or loved ones they have lost. Life is filled with trials, losses, and death, and many people do mourn over these things. But these have nothing to do with the kingdom of God and its work within the human realm. This mourning is spiritual in nature, not worldly or emotional.
    - The reason these "blessed" people are mourning is because of the pain and damage their sins have caused, and the fact that their sins are why Jesus went to His cross. This mourning is also for all the time, energy, and attention that has been lost on committing and then dealing with the fallout of their sins. This is time, energy, and attention that could have been devoted to God's work instead of their own selfish agenda.
    - And if it is not their own sins for which they mourn, it is over

sin itself, and all the damage and loss it has caused (2 Cor. 7:8–10). This loss is not calculated only in the number of souls separated from God (now and in eternity) but also the great destruction inflicted upon innocent children, animal life, and the physical world. There is plenty to mourn over when one begins contemplating the scale of this damage. Those who recognize this and do mourn "shall be comforted" by "the God of all comfort" (2 Cor. 1:3–5).

- ***"Blessed are the gentle, for they shall inherit the earth"*** (Mat. 5:5). "Gentle" in older translations is "meek," which many think means weak, timid, or even afraid. Yet Jesus, in the only time He described Himself, said *of* Himself that He is "gentle [or, meek] and humble in heart" (Mat. 11:29), which is exactly what He has just said of citizens of His kingdom.
  - Meekness usually means not retaliating in kind. It is a natural human tendency to hate those who hate us, curse those who curse us, show road rage to those who cut us off in traffic, spite those who did us wrong, etc. Meekness says, "I'm not going to lower myself to that person's level. I am going to take the high road here—even to my own hurt."
  - Selfish anger, domination, retaliation, and vengeance have no place in the kingdom of God. Jesus absorbed the losses He incurred as our Redeemer (1 Peter 2:21–23) by deferring to God's handling of His situation rather than taking matters into His own hands. This is what gentle/meek people do: they do not seek to vindicate themselves or enact their own justice, but they turn everything over to God.
  - Another aspect of gentle or meek people is that they are teachable. Being humble in heart and receptive to God's way of dealing with offenders, their heart is open to whatever the King teaches them. He is their Master; they are happy to be His students; they embrace His teaching as the path of love, light, and truth.
  - Jesus says that such people "will inherit the earth." This is likely a proverbial statement as we see in Mat. 16:26 ("gains the

whole world"). It seems that what Jesus means here is that by gentleness/meekness the citizens of the kingdom will gain what the vengeful and spiteful sought but never achieved. These latter people wanted the world to be perfect, according to their own standard of justice. Citizens of the kingdom want the world to be perfect according to God's standard of justice. These citizens will be rewarded with a perfect world while the others will lose everything (see 1 Cor. 3:21–22 and Rev. 21:7). It does not mean, "They will live on earth forever," but "They will inherit the good life with God that all others forfeited."

- **"Blessed are those who hunger and thirst for righteousness, for they shall be satisfied"** (Mat. 5:6). Left to themselves, people often hunger and thirst for all the wrong things. We want our bellies filled with what tastes good rather than the bread of life. We want to slake our thirst with sodas, sugar-loaded juices, and beer rather than living water. We want, we want, we want, and yet this "wanting" is never satisfied because it caters to the human appetite rather than spiritual desires for love, light, and truth.
  - Citizens of the kingdom hunger and thirst for what the King and His kingdom are all about: righteousness. "Righteousness" means whatever is right (thus, morally pure, holy, and just) in God's sight. God is a righteous God (Rom. 1:17); Christ is a righteous Savior (1 John 2:1); the kingdom of God is a righteous kingdom. To seek righteousness is to seek the kingdom and vice versa (Mat. 6:33).
  - Instead of craving for what the world craves, citizens of God's kingdom crave for what God offers—really, for who God *is*. Christ feeds the soul, not the belly; He provides spiritual nourishment, not mere food. To believe and obey Him is food for the human soul (John 6:26–29).

- **"Blessed are the merciful, for they shall receive mercy"** (Mat. 5:7). Mercy spares an offender what he deserves, always in hopes of the offender's change of heart and rehabilitation. A person may have a legal right to punish his offender but restrains himself in anticipation of a better outcome.

- While meekness and gentleness bear up under injustices, we are to offer mercy as a gift. In gentleness, we endure; in mercy, we impart. As God shows mercy, and Jesus is a merciful King, so the citizens of His kingdom are to be merciful, forbearing, and forgiving (Col. 3:12–14). People are fallible, make mistakes, and are sometimes just evil. But people are also redeemable and can change.
- God offers mercy to give a person opportunity to avoid punishment, come to his senses, and seek reconciliation. We should want this for others as much as we want it from God for ourselves. "For judgment will be merciless to one who has shown no mercy; mercy triumphs over judgment" (James 2:13).

❏ ***"Blessed are the pure in heart, for they shall see God"*** (Mat. 5:8). The "heart" is one's mind, thoughts, motives, and principles by which he lives. A pure heart is one that is free from evil, corruption, and rebellion. Pure hearts also have pure thoughts, which are what pure hearts dwell upon (Phil. 4:8). Christ our King is pure, "and everyone who has [his] hope fixed on Him purifies himself, just as He is pure" (1 John 3:3). These people "will see God" in His favor; He will welcome them into the eternal kingdom.
- Purity is not merely a conformity to rules. Jesus did not say, "Blessed are the conformists" or "rule-keepers," although it is true that the pure in heart always seek to obey God's commandments. But purity itself is an internal transformation of one's mind that purges all sinful thoughts and intentions *and* consciously pursues holiness and sanctification. No amount of science, positive thinking, feel-good philosophy, sermons, or good works can purify one's heart. This action requires a believer's sincerity and obedient faith *and* God's grace—not one or the other but both. God helps us only when we do not refuse His help.
- Those who are pure in heart will also be pure (right, just, honorable, transparent, etc.) in their actions (Psalm 24:3–4). The kingdom of God will not tolerate impurity; the King will not admit one who chooses to remain impure. "For this you

know with certainty, that no immoral or impure person or covetous man, who is an idolater, has an inheritance in the kingdom of Christ and God" (Eph. 5:5).

- ❑ ***"Blessed are the peacemakers, for they shall be called sons of God"*** (Mat. 5:9). Peace, like purity, is a fundamental characteristic of the kingdom of God. This does not mean that the kingdom cannot be at war, for it most certainly is, but that peace is its natural state and its goal in the event of war. Peacemakers, therefore, are those who at peace with God because they have been cleansed by Christ's blood and thus reconciled to Him (Col. 1:19).
  - Jesus never taught "peace at any price"—at the expense of everything else. He never taught us to pursue peace rather than, or in the place of, righteousness, for heavenly peace is never in conflict with heavenly righteousness. **First**, one must be at peace with God which is only possible through a covenant relationship with Him based upon one's faith and His grace (Rom. 5:1–2). **Second**, one must be at peace within, being content with God's grace and that person's standing with Him. **Third**, one must demonstrate this inward spiritual peace in his outward personal life, which is where "peacemaker" comes in.
  - Peacemakers are not passive people; they actively conduct themselves in such a way that promotes harmony and conciliation. "Pursue peace with all men" (Heb. 12:14) because peace is a pursuit, not a static trait. "If possible, so far as it depends on you, be at peace with all men" (Rom. 12:18). Peace may not always *be* possible; but when it is, Paul says, the kingdom citizen—who is also a son of God—is to take the initiative.

- ❑ ***"Blessed are those who have been persecuted for the sake of righteousness, for theirs is the kingdom of heaven"*** (see Mat. 5:10–12). The word "persecute" is from a Greek word meaning "to follow after (someone or something)."[88] It can be used positively (as in Phil. 3:14, "I *press on*"—same Greek word) or negatively (as Jesus used it here). The negative usage implies harassment, oppression, or punishment of someone for their beliefs (often religious or political).

- In the present case, "for the sake of righteousness" and "for My name's sake"—not two different "sakes" but the same one expressed in two ways—modify or qualify the kind of persecution Jesus meant. Anyone can be persecuted for even the most ridiculous beliefs or lifestyle choices. But children of the kingdom will be persecuted as a direct result of their faith in and obedience to their King, the Lord Jesus Christ. He does not give you or me the right to choose *why* we are persecuted: He has already chosen this; we (Christians) have already agreed to it. He will not reward the kingdom of heaven for any other kind of persecution.

- This last Beatitude is a hard sell. Americans are conditioned to believe that the absence of suffering is the route to happiness. Pain and suffering are to be alleviated at all costs, not accepted as part of one's spiritual outlook. Yet the NT states repeatedly how trials of faith and secular opposition are not only possible but expected (2 Tim. 3:12). The believer should "not be surprised… if the world hates you" (1 John 3:13), for the godless world hates everyone and everything that calls attention (directly or indirectly) to its ungodliness. God finds favor with those persecuted for their faith in Christ rather than those who suffer because of their sins (1 Peter 4:12–19).

- A virtuous life—a kingdom life—will draw attention because it is so markedly different from the rest of the world. Some of this attention will be good as people seek to have what the citizen of the kingdom has. Other attention will be negative as people who do not know God want to silence, cancel, and even destroy those who challenge their own beliefs. "[I]t is precisely in suffering that the people of God are selected; in suffering are they known. The tragedy of the times, therefore, becomes to us a personal summons to decide for the calling of God and, in tragedy, to serve Him."[89]

These eight statements characterize the heart and conduct of a citizen of God's kingdom. Regardless of what the world looks for in a person, these are the things the King looks for to participate in His kingdom work. The kingdom life is a blessed life: when one's heart is aligned with God's kingdom, blessings follow. This thought is not isolated to Jesus' sermon on the mount. Consider Paul's detail of kingdom activity in Rom. 12:9–21. Nothing he wrote there is at odds with what Jesus said on the mountain. Consider also what Peter said:

> To sum up, all of you be harmonious, sympathetic, brotherly, kindhearted, and humble in spirit; not returning evil for evil or insult for insult, but giving a blessing instead; for you were called for the very purpose that you might inherit a blessing. (1 Peter 3:8–9)

Peter's words here are the Beatitudes in a nutshell. He says exactly what Jesus said but in different words and in a Christian context. Whatever Jesus taught the Jews in preparation for entrance into the kingdom, so His apostles taught Christians to this same end.

Thus, we do not have two separate kingdom teachings—one for Jews and another for Christians—but a singular, unified, and completely consistent one. The Law of Moses has been fulfilled and is no longer binding; God's covenant with Israel has been fulfilled and a new one has taken its place. But whatever is necessary for entrance into God's kingdom remains unchanged under any law and in any covenantal context.

Summary Thoughts: The Beatitudes—the statements of blessedness—that open Jesus' sermon on the mount serves as the Ten Commandments of the kingdom. These also are built upon love: God's love for us and our love for God. Those who love God will be humble in heart, for no one can come to God while filled with pride. They will mourn for their sin and what it cost Jesus to remove that sin. These people will be meek and gentle, as Jesus was. They will hunger and thirst for righteousness, for this is the food and drink of the kingdom.

They will be merciful because God has been merciful to them. They will cleanse their hands of sin, purge their thoughts of evil, and purify their hearts for service in God's kingdom. They will be at peace with God and therefore will seek to be peacemakers with their fellow human beings whenever possible.

And yes, they will be persecuted for the sake of Christ and righteousness. Suffering for Christ's sake is appropriate since He has suffered so much for us. Suffering for what is right is part of kingdom living, at least while the age of the kingdom operates concurrently with the age of the world. These two kingdoms are in active conflict with each other; the citizens of each kingdom will also be in conflict.

In the afterlife, only the kingdom of God will survive and extend into eternity; all other kingdoms will be destroyed. So then, "momentary, light affliction is producing for us an eternal weight of glory far beyond all comparison, while we look not at the things which are seen, but at the things which are not seen; for the things which are seen are temporal, but the things which are not seen are eternal" (2 Cor. 4:17–18).

Chapter Twelve

The Kingdom of Love, Light, and Truth

Morally, the world is a mess. (It is a mess in other ways, too, but its *moral* mess is the root of all other messes.) Sin has corrupted God's pristine Creation, defiling the best of that Creation (human beings) to the point where it has become "utterly sinful" (Rom. 7:13). The human world is enveloped in moral, spiritual, and satanic darkness. Respect for God, His authority, His word, and whatever He deems sacred has been trampled underfoot by an untold number of unbelievers.

This is not a new thing. The Gentile kingdoms we discussed earlier—Babylon, Medo-Persia, Greece, and Rome—were comprised of people who worshiped false gods, practiced idolatry, and refused to give the God of heaven His deserved glory. They believed in foolish things and acted in ignorance; "Professing to be wise, they became fools" (Rom. 1:21–22). Their kingdoms practiced superstition, the occult, magic, sorcery, and divination. They devalued human life, committed crimes against humanity, and were often barbaric in their subjugation of lesser nations.

Things are no better today. People still worship false gods (though the depiction of these gods has changed), practice idolatry, and refuse to give God thanks or glory. Today, many people profess to be wise in their humanistic, secularized, and mechanical view of life, yet from a heavenly perspective they are fools, having been seduced by Satan, the greatest fool of all. Today people still dabble in (or are completely given over to) all sorts of evil thinking and evil behavior. People still devalue human life; abortion, murder, exploitation, atrocities, crimes against humanity, persecution, etc. are still rampant. Just because it is not happening in your neighborhood (though it probably is) does not mean that the world has not been infected with sin, moral perversity, and satanic deception.

That is the bad news. Here is very good news: God is still in control. He is not in control of all the evil, as though He is the source of it or responsible for it. On the other hand, all the evil in the world cannot change, corrupt, or undo God's righteous oversight of His Creation. While it appears that God is doing little or nothing to stop the onslaught of evil as it steamrolls innocent victims and helpless people, this is not true. Quite the opposite. We have no idea how awful the world would become overnight if God were to remove His providential restraints and other preventive measures within the human realm. We must not judge Him according to our expectations. Satan hates the world, and all that God has created. It is likely that, in the absence of God's restraining him, he would mercilessly kill everyone.

Here is even better news: God has given all control of His kingdom to His Son, Jesus Christ. I say "better" not to diminish God's majesty whatsoever, but only because now we have someone reigning over God's kingdom that understands our plight (Heb. 4:14–16). He has been one of us; He has walked this earth, seen with human eyes the plague of sin, and personally confronted human wickedness and even Satan himself. He has done all this not with timidity, uncertainty, or hand-wringing, but courageously, virtuously, and victoriously. God's greatest blessing to the world was to give His Son to us as a gift from heaven so that we might be saved through all that He accomplished (John 3:16).

Power struggles, conflicts of interest, and personal greed always compromise the kingdoms of men. Add to this the human flaws and sinful conditions of those who lead them, and we realize that, left to themselves, nothing good can or will come from all this. It is only when people, governments, and nations adopt the morals and virtues of God's kingdom do they flourish and succeed in a context where everyone benefits. This is because God's kingdom is inherently good and just, and its reigning King (Christ) is also good and just. This is exactly what God predicted seven hundred years before the human birth of His Son:

> Pay attention to Me, O My people, and give ear to Me, O My nation; for a law will go forth from Me, and I will set My justice

> for a light of the peoples. My righteousness is near, My salvation has gone forth, and My arms will judge the peoples … Lift up your eyes to the sky, then look to the earth beneath; for the sky will vanish like smoke, and the earth will wear out like a garment and its inhabitants will die in like manner; but My salvation will be forever, and My righteousness will not wane. (Isa. 51:4–6)

God's kingdom does not devalue people but raises them to where they could never be otherwise. It provides heavenly knowledge, wisdom, and revelation that has changed the world forever in a positive direction.

The initial effects of God's kingdom might be described as both inspiration and influence. When people learn about God—this refers to *accurate* information, as He has revealed Himself to us in His word—they are inspired by this knowledge. They begin seeing the world differently, and not just "the world" but also *their* world. They consciously appeal to a higher, transcendent value system that does not originate from human wisdom. Instead of merely thinking "what is the right thing to do?" they think "what is *right*, period?" This new set of values, based upon heavenly knowledge and wisdom, begins having its effect upon their heart.

This latter "effect" is the kingdom's influence. Once a person sees the world (and his world) through a different lens, he ideally begins to operate within that mental and spiritual framework. Before, he lied and thought little of it; he fornicated, and it did not bother him; he committed little thefts now and then, and it never stabbed his conscience. Now, however, having been inspired by a heavenly overview and influenced by its transcendent moral system, he is conscious of his lies, sexual sins, and thefts. He can no longer practice these without feeling the pang of guilt—not just feelings of regret, but *guilt* against the God of heaven.

This does not mean this person will immediately or automatically become a follower of Christ. Many people believe in God and His morality without committing to following His Son. All Christians are moralists, but not all moralists are Christians. But this is where the kingdom of God begins permeating the world of human sin, not to tolerate it or contentedly coexist with it, but to destroy it, one person at a time. For this reason, Jesus came into a sinful world as a single stone against a great statue of human sin, ready to "destroy the works of the devil" (1 John 3:8) while saving the souls overtaken by him.[90]

The kingdom of God is a kingdom of love. Love is what motivated God to create human beings, so that they could be a people of His own possession (Titus 2:14). Love is what motivated Him to give us free will, so that we could choose to serve Him above all else. Love is what motivated Him to send His Son, and for His Son to choose to enter our world and die on a cross, so that we could be rescued from all our poor decisions we rendered in that free will.

> "God is love" (1 John 4:8)—not merely loving, or lovable, but love is His divine *very nature*. Human love, left uninspired or unconditioned by divine influence, always falls short of and is inferior to God. We can imitate God's love but cannot duplicate it; God did not learn how to love by watching us (or, by His experience with us, as a mother learns to love her child) but we learn how to love supremely by watching Him. God's love is the source of all Christian love, never the other way around; all love that contradicts God's love also contradicts His own holy nature since "God is love." Love is not a mere nicety or pious virtue that God hopes Christians will embrace; rather, it is the foundational premise upon which all other laws and principles rest (Rom. 13:8–10, Gal. 5:13–14). Love is the "royal law" of the kingdom of God (James 2:8), the King Himself having demonstrated it to us in full (1 John 4:9–10).[91]

As God loves us, so we are to love one another. This "one another" phrase in the NT almost invariably refers to the brotherhood of believers in Christ, not to people in general. Love is the law of the kingdom, and therefore it is the law of the brotherhood.[92] Anyone who refuses to love his brother or sister in Christ stands in violation of the kingdom and the brotherhood. And anyone who loves his brother or sister in Christ has learned how to love those outside of Christ as well.

The people of God are a community knit to one another by its bond with the covenant God. It is a brotherhood, for within it all human relationships are regulated by the righteous law of that God; and all stand equally under that law. The covenant is not mechanical, following the natural course of things; it is a bilateral, moral agreement and can be voided. It is "a bond in blood sovereignly administered"[93]; it is "an elected, as opposed to natural, relationship of obligation established under divine sanction."[94] Mistreatment of a brother violates God's covenant, for he who does so "spits on the law of God and, in that fact, does not keep covenant with Him."[95]

The kingdom of God is a kingdom of light. "Light" was the first thing God gave to the newly created "heavens and earth" (Gen. 1:1–5). Bible commentators sometimes refer to the physical world (including humankind) as the "old" Creation, which is material in nature. The "new" creation is the result of the Light of the world (Christ) coming into the heart of a believer and bringing about a spiritual change in him. "God is Light, and in Him there is no darkness at all" (1 John 1:5). Likewise, God's kingdom is Light, and God's Son is "the Light of the world" who brings "the light of life" into every believer (John 8:12). All the positive characteristics of light—truth, vision, clarity, knowledge, wisdom, perspective, etc.—are part of this enlightenment.

The kingdom is, in effect, heaven coming down to earth, enveloping the darkened world of sin with a message of redemption, reconciliation with God, and hope. There is no coincidence between this and what we see in Christ: He came down to earth, "and the people who walk in darkness [saw] a great light" (Isa. 9:2; compare Mat. 4:16). Jesus the King is also the Light of the world, and, as with the Father, in Him there is no darkness at all (John 1:9).

The kingdom of God is a kingdom of truth. Truth requires authority, for nothing can be true apart from an authority that declares it so. (This point is not limited to religious or biblical truth.) As the King over God's kingdom, Christ *is* "the truth," having full endorsement from His Father, the highest source of authority that exists (John 14:6). This truth—really, Christ Himself—will make us free (John 8:31–32). Ignorance and moral darkness blind people to the truth; God's kingdom reveals the truth about God, Christ, our souls, salvation, and the afterlife. It promotes this truth throughout the world through the gospel of Christ.

Truth is inseparable from righteousness because nothing can be righteous to God unless it is true, and whatever God declares to be true is also right because He cannot lie (Titus 1:2). When we consider the word of God to be true, we must not mean "It is true to *me*," because you are not the standard for any truth outside of your own (which is really your opinion, not "truth"). In the end, it does not matter what is true to you or me, it only matters what God *declares* is true. The kingdom of God does not operate based on your truth or my truth, but God's truth (which is the only truth that will exist in the world to come).

Redemption, Restoration, Renewal: The kingdom of God is all about redemption, restoration, and renewal. These are the reasons why God has disclosed it to us. These are its objectives as it operates in the human realm. These objectives are both spiritual and practical: by spiritually transforming human hearts, those who are transformed begin living as citizens of the kingdom. These then become the "salt" and "light" of the world—testifiers of what God's goodness has done for them—and bring a message of love, hope, and salvation to others. This is the intention of God's kingdom, to produce living witnesses of its heavenly influence to transform hardened sinners into holy saints.

> In their treatment of the age to come, the Gospels' primary interest is ... restoration of fellowship with God. The pure in heart will see God (Mat. 5:8) and enter into the joy of their Lord (25:21, 23). The harvest will take place and the grain will be gathered into the barn (13:30, 39; Mark 4:29; cf. Mat. 3:12; Rev. 14:15). The sheep will be separated from the goats and brought safely into the fold (Mat. 25:32). The most common picture

is that of a feast or table fellowship. Jesus will drink wine again with His disciples in the kingdom of God (Mark 14:25). They will eat and drink at Jesus' table in the kingdom (Luke 22:30). The consummation is likened to a wedding feast (Mat. 22:1–14; 25:1–12) and a banquet (8:11; Luke 14:16–24). All these metaphors picture the restoration of communion between God and mankind that had been broken by sin.[96]

Jesus' stated mission was "to seek and save the lost" (Luke 19:10). The "lost" are those alienated from God because of their sin, their failure to keep their covenant with God (in the case of the Jews), and their ignorance of God (in the case of the Gentiles). Jesus wants these lost people to be found; it will be His kingdom mission to find them, inspire them, and influence them, in hopes that His message of love and hope will convert them. To be "found" is to be reconciled to God through the teachings of the kingdom (which are consistent with the teachings of Christ's gospel).

The kingdom of God is all about *eternal life*. The gospels record an account of a rich young ruler coming to Jesus (Mat. 19:16–26). This wealthy young man sought to "obtain eternal life," and wanted Jesus' endorsement of his credentials, as he saw them. Jesus listed off several key commandments from the Law of Moses, and the man claimed to have kept all of them. But when Jesus told him to sell everything and follow Him, "he went away grieving; for he was one who owned much property." Thus, Jesus did not confirm his expectations. Or he expected Jesus to tell him to do something relatively simple that he could knock out easily enough.

Instead, Jesus told him the "plain and unvarnished truth about himself."[97] He pointed out the real flaw in his heart, thinking, and life; He exposed him, thus forcing himself to be confronted with what He exposed. The problem was not intellectual, as though one could reason his way out of it, but moral and spiritual. The man asked, in essence, "What good deed must I do that I haven't done?" And Jesus, instead of pointing to any one good deed, said in essence, "Leave behind who you are and come, let Me make you into something far better."

But what captures our attention is this: the rich young ruler sought "eternal life," and Jesus responded with, "it is hard ... to enter the kingdom of heaven." Jesus put "eternal life" and entrance into the kingdom on the same page, on the same level, and as being the same pursuit. Whoever seeks the kingdom seeks life with God; whoever seeks life with God must do so through kingdom-seeking, not merely good works or pious living.

Who has Jesus invited into this kingdom life? Anyone who is lost; thus, anyone who needs to be saved. God is a redeeming God, a restoring God, and a God of renewal. Those who are lost need exactly what He has to offer them. Christ's kingdom exerts its power and influence to reach those who are lost to bring them back into a right relationship with God, to restore the innocence they once forfeited in sin.

> In His preaching Jesus regularly invited people to enter the kingdom of God, that is, to open their lives to the ruling of God. It is important to notice whom He invited. He invited everyone. That is the great surprise. He did not restrict the invitation to the respectable people, or the religious, or the wealthy or powerful (in Jesus' day wealth and power were often thought to be signs of God's blessing). Jesus included everyone without distinction. He spoke of God sending His servants out to highways and hedges to urge people to come in to the kingdom. He even said that it is more difficult for the rich to enter the kingdom than for a camel to go through the eye of a needle (Mat. 19:24). He said that the tax-collectors and prostitutes would go into the kingdom before the moral and religious people (Mat. 21:31). In brief, God is very gracious and loving toward all people, and His kingdom is offered to everyone.[98]

The kingdom's objective, however, is not only to save people's souls but to transform the saved into "a people for God's own possession, zealous for good deeds" (Titus 2:14). In the Law of Moses, sin always had to be taken care of first, then consecration—never the other way around. This is why, though consecratory burnt offerings are mentioned first in *Leviticus*, it is the sin offerings that are *made* first (sequentially). This is the kingdom's agenda: first, take care of sin, then begin reconditioning the heart of those who are forgiven so they can live like forgiven people. These people are then brought together with others who are going through the same transformation—fellow Christians who assemble regularly (Acts 2:42).

> Jesus employed the phrase kingdom of God or of heaven to indicate that perfect order of things which he was about to establish, in which all those of every nation who should believe in him were to be gathered together into one society, dedicated and intimately united to God, and made partakers of eternal salvation. This kingdom is spoken of as now begun and actually present inasmuch as its foundations have already been laid by Christ and its benefits realized among men that believe in him.[99]

This "one society" is Christ's church, a spiritual assembly of redeemed souls that, while on earth, serve the King in various ministries. These people have "put on the Lord Jesus Christ" and have "clothed [themselves] with Christ" (Rom. 13:14 and Gal. 3:27), which is to say that they are clothed with the King's clothes. They increasingly conform to the King (Rom. 8:29), and "walk in the same manner as He walked" (1 John 2:6). They walk about the earth as ambassadors of the King, offering words of kindness, acts of benevolence, and prayers of intercession. It is the highest honor to represent the King of all Creation to those made in His image (Gen. 1:27).

We are speaking, of course, in ideal terms. Not everyone who is baptized into Christ will honor their commitment to Him; sadly, the retention rate is low, the walk-away rate is high. Even so, this does not impede the progress of the kingdom or its influence throughout the world of human activity. God does far more than we will ever know; we should not limit His ability or activity only to what we know or imagine. Even though proportionately few will remain faithful to the King throughout their entire lives, He can do great things with these few people, just as He can do great things with a mustard seed-sized faith (Mat. 17:20).

Numbers and percentages do not impede God's purposes or plans. The kingdom of God is about power, not words, numbers, and statistics (1 Cor. 4:20). He can preach through Noah, a righteous man whose faith in God condemned the world; He can also preach through Judas as he dangled from the tree where he took his own life.

A New Creation: In embracing the kingdom's love, light, and truth, the believer dies to himself, his world, and his former allegiance to sin and is reborn ("born again") into a new state of being. He is baptized into Christ, the water of baptism serving as a visible and historical transition from one life to the other. This new state of being produces a newness of life, newness of heart, and a daily renewal of his spirit. He is no longer merely a personage of the human realm; he has become a citizen of God's kingdom.

We see this transformation detailed in the following passages:

- "There was the true Light which, coming into the world, enlightens every man" (John 1:9).
- "But as many as received Him, to them He gave the right to become children of God, even to those who believe in His name, who were born, not of blood nor of the will of the flesh nor of the will of man, but of God" (John 1:12–13).
- "Jesus answered, 'Truly, truly, I say to you, unless one is born of water and the Spirit he cannot enter into the kingdom of God'" (John 3:5).
- "Therefore if anyone is in Christ, he is a new creature; the old things passed away; behold, new things have come" (2 Cor. 5:17).
- "Do not lie to one another, since you laid aside the old self with its evil practices, and have put on the new self who is being renewed to a true knowledge according to the image of the One who created him" (Col. 3:9–10).
- "for in this way [i.e., by supplying your faith] the entrance into the eternal kingdom of our Lord and Savior Jesus Christ will be abundantly supplied to you" (2 Peter 1:11, bracketed words added).

The kingdom of light illuminates the human soul, filling it with God's love, truth, heavenly knowledge, and divine assurance. This light, once internalized, radiates outward in the believer's life, conditioning his attitude, recalibrating his thinking, and overflowing into his relationships. Because he walks with Christ in fellowship, he also enjoys fellowship with all others who also walk with Christ. His eyes are on Christ (Col. 3:1–3); his heart is where his treasure is—in heaven (Mat. 6:20–21); his citizenship is in heaven (Phil. 3:20–21).

Again, this is an idealized picture. Along the way, this believer (like all believers) will wrestle with doubts, struggle against the darkness of this world, battle temptations, and at times fail. He will face trials, tragedies, losses, and defeats; he will often be strong in his faith and at times experience periods of weakness. While God's kingdom is perfect, and its King is perfect, its citizens are not. This is a matter of fact, not a matter of choice: the believer must never choose to be imperfect, but because he is human, he is inherently so. He will spend the rest of his life *being* perfected—in his faith, in his walk, and in his love. In his ever-perfecting love, he will draw ever nearer to God and have no fear of the judgment to come (James 4:8, 1 John 4:17–18).

Having become a citizen *of* the kingdom, the believer then becomes a participant *in* the kingdom. Citizens do not merely occupy a space on a pew or an entry on a roster; they are actively involved in promoting the kingdom in whatever manner God has so equipped them. Citizens are servants, never spectators; they respond to the call of duty, not the siren call of the world. No one can serve in God's kingdom who has not yet done what God requires of him to become its citizen. On the other hand, God is gracious to give citizenship to anyone who will love and obey His Son (the King).

Summary Thoughts: The world is a mess, but God's world is beautiful and flawless. His kingdom of Light brings God's inspiration and influence into the world, one believer at a time. The entire human race since the time of Christ has been positively affected by these things. Yes, there have been many who have had erroneous ideas about God, His kingdom, and His church, and they have acted poorly based upon those ideas. However, God's work in the human world continues unabated and searches out those who are seeking the truth.

As stated earlier, the kingdom's (and its King's) objective is not just to save people from sin but also to transform them into productive servants of God. This transformation comes through the renewing of one's mind, having no longer conformed to the inferior and corrupted image of this world (Rom. 12:1–2). God's kingdom is characterized by love, light, and truth; its objectives are redemption, restoration, and renewal. Just as "God is Light," those who become citizens of this kingdom are spiritually illuminated and renewed with heavenly wisdom.

God's kingdom is the power and authority behind all such illumination, transformation, and salvation. This power and authority are embodied in the King Himself (Christ) who reigns with perfect wisdom and ability over all that has come into existence. The purpose for this reign is to bring souls to God and give meaning to the "old" Creation by saving from it those who are brought into a "new" creation: Christians.

Chapter Thirteen

Seeking First the Kingdom

In Mat. 6:25–32, Jesus spoke rhetorically about how people fret over their daily needs, typified by food, water, and clothing. He made a point about how God feeds the birds of the air every day; if God can do this for birds, why can He not also do this for people? If God can clothe flowers, why can He not also clothe people?

Jesus' point was for His people to focus on their faith in the God who provides rather than worry about their earthly needs or circumstances. Of course, this is often easier said than done—and He knew this—but such perspective is that of kingdom living. Citizens of the kingdom do not doubt the provisions of their King; they have higher and nobler concerns. They do not occupy all their time acquiring things that God has already promised to provide; they have greater pursuits.

The essence of these concerns and pursuits is summed up in Mat. 6:33: "But seek first His kingdom and His righteousness, and all these things will be added to you." Jesus did not say, "God will take care of these things regardless of *whether* you seek the kingdom" but *because* you do so. God "is a rewarder of those who seek Him" (Heb. 11:6), and part of His reward in this life is the providential care of His people.

But what does this mean, to "seek first the kingdom"?

Seeking the Kingdom: We know that the kingdom of God under the leadership of His Son is the Father's answer to our fallen world and our own fallenness. Jesus wants us to stay focused on this great redemption and His wise and capable leadership of our lives. He does not want us distracted with things that God has already promised to take care of—earthly needs, daily provisions, clothing, etc.

Being distracted is an easy thing to do, of course, which requires us to be diligent and strenuous in this focus. The world—not just the morally evil world, but *this life*—has a tremendous pull on our attention. It takes great effort to overcome this draining effect on our faith.

The word "seek" in Mat. 6:33 has an ever-present tense to it. This means keep on seeking; do not just seek once (or occasionally) but keep seeking the kingdom as a matter of daily living. Christians may be great seekers on Sunday morning in the middle of a church service, but this is not what Jesus meant. As God's kingdom is important to God, it must also be important to His people. Earlier in the chapter, Jesus taught us to pray, "Your will be done on earth as it is in heaven" (Mat. 6:10). We are to see ourselves as participants in carrying out that will, not requesting that it be done apart from us.

Seekers are active lookers, searchers, and pursuers. While kingdom seekers will certainly assemble with fellow believers, churchgoing is no replacement for kingdom-seeking. The man who sought his lost sheep in Jesus' parable did not sit at home or attend a church service to do this. He went after it with a sense of concern, mission, and urgency. Likewise, the woman who lost one of ten coins became a conscious and active seeker of that lost coin (Luke 15:1–10). Neither person stopped searching until they found what they were looking for.

Likewise, our seeking the kingdom of God is to be perpetual and persistent. Jesus links this seeking mindset to prayer: we ask, we seek, we knock (Mat. 7:7–8). We ask God questions, for wisdom, or for better understanding. Then we actively seek after what we have asked for, which brings us to a door of opportunity and enlightenment. We knock on this door and God opens it for us. This is the pattern of spiritual growth; this is how we grow in Christ.

But what are we looking for? We are seekers for the things of God: His love, His light, and His truth. We seek heavenly things more importantly than earthly things. We seek redemption from our sinful decisions and deliverance from battles with temptation. We seek deeper fellowship with God through Christ, drawing near to Him with trusting faith. We seek ways to serve our fellow believers and our fellow human beings. We seek the lost for the sake of bringing more people into God's kingdom. We seek whatever God wishes to show us; whatever He wants us to discover about Him and His word.

We seek Him firstly ("seek first"), which implies putting the priority of the search for Him above all other priorities and searches. It implies putting God's business ahead of our own, making His concerns our concerns. "First in our affections, first in the objects of pursuit, first in the feelings and associations of each morning, be the desire and the aim for heaven. Having this, we have assurance of all we need. God, our Father, will then befriend us; and in life and death all will be well."[100]

We cannot hail Christ as our King but then relegate Him and His work to a small segment of our lives. He needs to have our first attention; He wants His kingdom to be more important to us than our own personal kingdoms. There can be no competition here, no rivalry, no divided heart. "No one can serve two masters" (Mat. 6:24), and no one can serve two kingdoms.

And His Righteousness: Jesus adds "His righteousness" in what we are to seek (Mat. 6:33). There is no contradiction here, no choosing between "kingdom" and "righteousness." They are the same pursuit: as we seek one, we are also seeking the other. When we seek righteousness (i.e., what God says is right, true, and holy), our pursuit will lead us to the kingdom and its concerns. When we seek the kingdom, our pursuit will lead us to righteous living. These two things are never in conflict; they never lead us in two different directions.

Righteousness is a divine attribute. This means it speaks to God's inherent and immutable (unchanging) character. He can never be anything less than righteous; He cannot deny Himself those attributes that define His essential nature (2 Tim. 2:13). The apostle Peter fittingly identified Christ as "the Righteous One" (Acts 3:14); the apostle John identified our Advocate with God as "Jesus Christ the righteous" (1 John 2:1).

As Christ is righteous, so are His people, having been cleansed by His blood to engage in the work of His kingdom. "We must also 'seek first His kingdom and His righteousness' (Mat. 6:33). What is the object of our quest? The Church? Heaven? No; we are to seek God's righteousness—His sway, His rule, His reign in our lives."[101]

> Men and women were meant to live as God made them to live. They were meant to live to His glory and to keep His commandments. They were meant to be upright; to be pure and clean and honest and noble. They were put on their feet so that they might look into the face of God and enjoy His companionship. That is righteousness.[102]

The Jewish scribes and Pharisees in Jesus' day thought they had cornered the market on righteousness. They prided themselves on this, even boasted about it (Luke 18:9). Yet their view was skewed, self-serving, and frequently modified to fit their own circumstances (consider Mark 7:9–13, for example). They were religious professionals, professors of theology, and the final authority for all things having to do with the Law and its interpretations.

Yet Jesus was not impressed. "For I say to you that unless your righteousness surpasses that of the scribes and Pharisees, you will not enter the kingdom of heaven" (Mat. 5:20). This was an amazing statement, as the people held the Pharisees in high regard and closer to God than themselves.[103] Even so, the righteousness of the kingdom of God was not only better than the Pharisees' self-determined righteousness; it was different altogether. Someone has said that the kingdom's righteousness is not just a higher rung than theirs but a different ladder on a different wall. "The righteousness which God requires is the righteousness of God's kingdom which God imparts as He comes to rule within our lives."[104]

"The righteous man shall live by faith" (Rom. 1:17): since we have sinned against God and therefore have no righteousness of our own, He credits us with righteous when we exercise obedient faith in Him. This righteousness is "apart from works" (Rom. 4:6), meaning it is not based upon perfect performance, as we covered in an earlier chapter. Rather, it is based upon Christ's love, His uncorrupted virtue, and His perfect obedience. Our righteousness is possible only through His. Therefore, "by His doing you are in Christ Jesus, who became to us wisdom from God, and righteousness and sanctification, and redemption, so that, just as it is written, 'Let him who boasts, boast in the Lord'" (1 Cor. 1:30–31).

Seeking God "in Christ": "If Christ is in you, though the body is dead because of sin, yet the spirit is alive because of righteousness" (Rom. 8:10). For Christ to be in you, you must first be in Him. The NT phrase "in Christ" (and its variations—"in Him," "in Jesus Christ," etc.) always means the same thing: in a covenant relationship with God through Christ. Or we could say: in fellowship with the Father through the mediation of His Son (1 Cor. 1:9). Or: made citizens of God's kingdom through faith in its King, Jesus Christ. In any case, there needs to be a known and viable agreement between the two parties (God and you), with Christ as mediator (1 Tim. 2:5).

To be "in Christ" has nothing to do with church buildings and worship services. It has to do with the disposition of your heart and the object of your faith. These two things (heart and faith) must agree, and both must simultaneously follow Christ the King. Kingdom fellowship is not determined by church attendance, church directories, church buildings, or church work. It is determined by your devotion to the King and His work, as one who is actively seeking to participate in this work.

"Therefore if anyone is in Christ, he is a new creature; the old things passed away; behold, new things have come" (2 Cor. 5:17). The "old things" are of this Creation, the carnal world, and sinful practices. "New things" are of the new creation which conforms to the Son, "who is the image of God" (2 Cor. 4:4), and the holy activity of His kingdom. The "old things" are of the age of this world; "new things" are of the age of the kingdom.

The new creation—what Paul calls elsewhere "the new self"—is made "according to the image of the One who created him" (Col. 3:10). Christians are *made* Christians not merely to sit on pews, sing songs, and listen to sermons. Rather, they have been "created in Christ Jesus for good works" (Eph. 2:10) that draw people's attention to what inspired them—the Father Himself (Mat. 5:16).

The Need for Repentance: What does this new creation "in Christ" look like? What does God expect of you? We must not overlook one essential requirement of those seeking the kingdom of God: repentance. Jesus preached, "The time is fulfilled, and the kingdom of God is at hand; repent and believe in the gospel" (Mark 1:15). There are several other passages in the gospel accounts like this. Repentance is not a subtopic of a discussion of the kingdom. Rather, no one can become its citizen who does not *first* and as needed *continually* repent of his sins.

Repentance is a change of heart *and* behavior—always in that order—that takes a person back to where he deviated from the path of righteousness. This does not mean that he regresses or turns backward in time. Instead, he commits to living as God had always intended, or he renews what he had once committed to ("repent and return"—Acts 3:19). Repentance requires "fruit," which is measurable, discernible, or visible proof of its existence (Mat. 3:8, Acts 26:20).

Repentance is not a feeling, emotion, or idea. It is a decision. It is the kingdom of God's demand of anyone who wishes to "come after" the King (Mat. 16:24, Mark 6:12).[105] After His resurrection, Jesus said to His disciples, "Thus it is written, that the Christ would suffer and rise again from the dead the third day, and that repentance for forgiveness of sins would be proclaimed in His name to all the nations, beginning from Jerusalem" (Luke 24:46–47).

Repentance is necessary for forgiveness; God's promise to forgive a person is based upon his decision to repent.

> God's Kingdom does not ask us to create the life that it requires; God's Kingdom will give us that life. God's Kingdom does not set up a standard and say, "When you achieve this standard of righteousness, you may enter the Kingdom." God's Kingdom makes one demand: Repent! Turn! Decide! Receive the Kingdom; for as you receive it you receive its life you receive its blessing, you receive the destiny reserved for those who embrace it.[106]

In this decision, there must be no room made for half-hearted commitment, reluctance, hesitation, clinging to what must be left behind, or grieving for what has passed (Luke 9:62). It is a decision—a difficult, urgent, full, and radical decision. Kingdom-seeking is always decision time. Righteous living is always decision time. These are not two separate decisions but the same: one decision requires that the other also be made.

In seeking God's kingdom and righteousness, a person must not carry with him either his past sins or present ones. He must leave these behind, walk away from them forever, and not make any provision for them in the future (Rom. 13:14). Difficult as this can be—Jesus likened it to gouging out one's right eye or severing his right hand (Mat. 5:29–30)—it is necessary if one wishes to become a citizen of the kingdom. We cannot seek the kingdom or God's righteousness otherwise. But if we do sincerely repent, He will welcome us and receive us into His kingdom—now in promise, later in full realization of that promise.

Repentance is not the only thing God expects of you, but it is one thing that Jesus explicitly states up front. He also requires water baptism and explicitly states this (Mat. 28:19). In the conversion process, repentance and baptism go together; one is useless without the other; one will not be accepted without the other (Acts 2:38). While the baptism of

John the Baptist accomplished different things than does the believer's baptism into Christ, they both converge on repentance (Luke 3:3).

Change, decision, repentance, commitment—these are all hard sells today. They go against human nature, comfort zones, and our modern perception of churchgoing religion. They comprise the path of most resistance, not the path of least resistance. In promising to follow Jesus the King, we promise to relinquish self-will and to pick up our cross of sacrifice and self-denial. Some Christians are successful at this; the rest of us struggle, resist, and even (at times) refuse to comply. Some churches are successful, others resist. Speaking especially of denominational religion (but with broad application), John Bright says:

> As for the cross of the Servant, it is not strange to us. ... We enthrone [our] crucified Saviour [sic] in stained glass, wood, and stone—and in doctrine. To that cross we look for salvation. But we want that cross not at all. Indeed we would have it the chief business of religion to keep crosses far away. We want a Christ who suffers that we may not have to, a Christ who lays Himself down that our comfort may be undisturbed. The call to lose life that it may be found again, to take up the cross and follow, remains mysterious and offensive to us. To be sure, we labor to bring men to Christ…but our labor we see as a labor of conquest and growth, successful programs and dollars. Can it be that we are seeking to build the Kingdom of the Servant—without following the Servant [Jesus Christ]? If we do so, we will doubtless build a great church—but will it have anything to do with the Kingdom of God?[107]

This is an uncomfortable admission. Christians are supposed to seek first the kingdom, not church services, church work, and church programs. I realize these things sound virtuous and noble up front, and at times may be so, but often these tend to push the kingdom's interests out of the way to make room for lesser things and human egos. We are not the King, but Christ is; we are not the head of Christ's church, but He is.

We must be careful not to turn secondary matters into primary ones, and primary matters into secondary ones. If we do so, we become no different than the Pharisees. They prided themselves on being "sons of the kingdom," wore their righteousness like a priestly robe, and proudly displayed phylacteries on their heads just as some Christians display crosses on golden chains around their necks.[108] Yet the Pharisees failed to see the kingdom in their midst and then crucified its King. And, sadly, some Christians may also fail to see the kingdom, being blinded by a church-bound religion.

Summary Thoughts: God takes care of those who trust in Him to do so. When we seek His kingdom, we enjoy His providential care, however He determines this. Our seeking is not a mere confession of faith, testimony of belief, or promise to obey. Rather, it is an active, continuous, and ever-productive pursuit of heavenly knowledge, spiritual understanding, and God Himself. This is the pursuit of one who first learns of the King; this is also the life of the citizen of His kingdom. We "seek first His kingdom" not because we do not know what it is but because we want to learn more about it and grow in that knowledge.

We seek not only the kingdom itself but also the righteousness that characterizes it. God is a righteous God; His Son is a righteous King; and His kingdom is a righteous kingdom. Kingdoms of men are fraught with internal problems, inconsistencies, moral deviations, and conflicts of interest.

God's kingdom has none of these things. There is nothing wrong about God or His kingdom; everything is perfect, flawless, and optimal. His kingdom not only is righteous in its design and its work, but it also produces righteous people when they conform to its King.

The kingdom of God calls for repentance. This was one of its primary messages when John the Baptist, Jesus, and the apostles unveiled it to us. It is no less important today. No one can enter the kingdom who refuses to repent of his sins. The King died to remove these sins and their power, not to perpetuate or justify them.

We honor the King when we willfully surrender our heart—and everything that is in our heart—to Him. We honor the kingdom when we conform to the moral teachings which define it. Repentance is often difficult, and change is usually inconvenient and uncomfortable, yet these actions are along the route to glory.

Chapter Fourteen

Working in the Kingdom

The kingdom of God is not Christ's church, and His church is not the kingdom. However, these two things are directly and necessarily related. This means that whatever a person does for one, he does for the other; contributing to one necessarily contributes to the other; commitment to one necessitates commitment to the other. And Christ's acceptance of a human soul to one necessarily implies His acceptance to the other.

I say all this to address two major misunderstandings about the kingdom and the church. The first misunderstanding is to make them the same thing—something I covered in detail in an earlier chapter. The second misunderstanding is to think that we need to pick and choose between the two things in our explanation of either one.

For example, if I say, "We are workers in God's kingdom," this does not make us any less workers in Christ's church (and vice versa). The same work can apply to both contexts, even though the contexts themselves remain independently identified. On the other hand, kingdom work may be a more accurate description of what is happening than church work.

Consider Jesus' parable of the sower (Mat. 13:1–23). This is a kingdom parable, not a church parable; it speaks to the "mysteries of the kingdom" (13:11), not the mysteries of the church. What is planted in each human heart is not the gospel of the church but the "word [or message] of the kingdom" (13:19). The "crop" that the "good soil" produces is not many converts to the church but an increase to the kingdom—an increase which may result in converts but can be understood in different ways as well.

We tend to think, and maybe have been conditioned to think, that this "crop" means souls added to the church because baptisms and church growth are how we tend to measure success. Church work is often visibly manifested in numbers, sermons, classes, converts, membership increases, etc. Kingdom work, however, does not rely upon these things.

For example, Paul's preaching in Athens resulted in very few converts for the church, yet his message about the "unknown God" was extremely successful, not only for the Athenians but also for us who read it two thousand years later. Paul never mentioned the church in his sermon, but he did speak of God as the King over all humankind *and* of the King's Son as the Judge of all humankind by virtue of His resurrection from the dead (Acts 17:24–31).

But, as said earlier, what benefits the one always benefits the other. An "increase of the heritage of the kingdom"—a phrase that has become part of traditional church vernacular—is also an increase of the church, in one form or another. Sometimes it is the kingdom worker's faith that increases; sometimes it is the church's membership that increases; and sometimes it is both. But always as a person contributes to one context (the kingdom), he always contributes in some form to the other (the church), and vice versa.

At the same time, the message of the King (Christ) and His kingdom (the kingdom of God) should not be an afterthought in our preaching, or something that converts learn about years after their conversion. The kingdom is the foundation for the church: Christ's power and authority (as King), as well as His love, mercy, and grace (as High Priest) are required for His church to exist and function. If He is not King, the church has no authority to exist; if He is not High Priest, the church cannot function as a sanctuary of redeemed souls.

This begs a question: how do we know if we are working in the kingdom (as faithful citizens to the King) or working in the church (as faithful members of Christ's body)? Jesus' parable of the talents (Mat. 25:14–30) is not about church work but is a parable about the kingdom (compare 25:1 and 25:14). Do we use our "talents"—whatever gifts, resources, or responsibilities to which God has entrusted us—for the kingdom or for the church? If we were to bury our "one talent" in the ground, do we forfeit the reward of the kingdom, or do we forfeit the reward of the church's future glory?

As I see it, these are not pointless questions. For most of my multi-decade Christian life, I have regarded my service to the Lord as church work, almost never as kingdom work. I rarely thought about myself as working for the kingdom. I have since reconsidered this, realizing now that much of what I was doing was in fact kingdom work conducted in a "church" context (i.e., as work for or that benefited a given congregation). I say this because so much of what I have done as a teacher, preacher, and writer of biblical studies was really to promote kingdom teaching, principles, and authority more so than specifically addressing church issues.

But then, it really does not matter. By expounding upon kingdom teaching, I have benefited my congregation. And by dealing with church issues, I have promoted kingdom teaching. I am not alone in this: many Christians have done the same thing, having followed the same path that I have followed. The fact that it took me so long to realize this is not flattering, yet I am glad to finally have this perspective now rather than not at all.

Kingdom Work Defined: How does a Christian support the kingdom, specifically? First, one does this by upholding Christ's authority. I know I have said a lot about authority in this book, and maybe some readers are tired of hearing about it, but if we do not know of and respect authority then we cannot be faithful Christians.

Truth requires authority: if Christ did not have the authority to embody in Himself God's truth, then He is a fraud and cannot save us (see John 8:31–32 and 14:6). If He does not have authority as the King over God's kingdom, then He cannot save us. If God has not authorized His Son as the head over His church, then He is an impostor and cannot save us.

People may not like to talk about authority because they would rather talk about love, grace, forgiveness, and inheritances, but all these things are useless without divine authority backing them up. For example, if Christ does not have the authority to forgive you, then He cannot in fact do so. He might claim to forgive you, but He lacks the right and power to make it happen. A primary reason for Christ reigning over the kingdom of God is so that He can exercise kingly authority for the salvation of your soul. If He did not have this, then "your faith is worthless; you are still in your sins" (1 Cor. 15:17).

Recognizing Christ's authority is necessary to obey Him. If you do not believe He has authority over you, or authority to save you, then you will not (and should not) obey Him. As it is, Jesus demonstrated His authority over all realms of nature as well as all spiritual realms. He walked on water, quieted the storm with His own voice, multiplied bread and fish to feed thousands of people, made a tree wither at His command, and healed "every kind of disease and every kind of sickness among the people" (Mat. 4:23). He also demonstrated His authority over the spiritual realm, in that angels attended Him and He cast out demons with His own command (Luke 4:36). And He demonstrated His authority over nature *and* the spiritual realm all at once whenever He raised someone from the dead (John 11:43–44).

Jesus Himself said, "If I do not do the works of My Father, do not believe Me; but if I do them, though you do not believe Me, believe the works, so that you may know and understand that the Father is in Me, and I in the Father" (John 10:37–38). This is not a church teaching but a kingdom teaching. Anyone can join a church and participate in a church-based religion. But no one is going to deny himself, take up his cross, and follow Jesus (Mat. 16:24) unless he believes that Jesus is a Man—indeed, also a divine Being—with supernatural authority.

Another way to support the kingdom is to adopt and practice its virtues. I expounded upon these in chapter eleven concerning the Beatitudes (Mat. 5:1–12). The Beatitudes are not church virtues but kingdom virtues; they do not express the heart of a mere churchgoer but the heart of one who worships the King; they do not define churchgoers but citizens of the kingdom—sons of God.

Many Christians will no doubt put on their best behavior for a church service or church-sponsored events (classes, meetings, etc.). But kingdom behavior is 24/7; it is not limited to a Sunday morning or a meeting place; it must not be conducted only in the company of other Christians. When Jesus said that we are to be the salt of the earth and light of the world, He was not talking about what we do in church buildings but *how we live as citizens of His kingdom* (Mat. 5:13–16). We are not to be "poor in spirit" (humble) only during a church service; we are to have this heart *all the time*. We are not to be hungry and thirsty for righteousness for the duration of a sermon; we are to crave righteousness *always* and in *all* circumstances.

If we adopt a heart prepared for kingdom service, then we will always be seeking to practice kingdom behavior. Paul said that we are to dwell (or meditate) upon godly virtues and then practice these in real life (Phil. 4:8–9). This is not a practice of the church as a collective organization (whether we are talking about the entire brotherhood or a single congregation) but of individual citizens of the kingdom. It is not surprising, then, that just prior to that instruction he wrote that "our citizenship is in heaven, from which also we eagerly wait for a Savior, the Lord Jesus Christ" (Phil. 3:20). This is not church talk; this is kingdom talk. The believer's citizenship is not in his congregation but in the kingdom of God over which Christ reigns as King.

Paul also tells us to "keep seeking the things above, where Christ is, seated at the right hand of God" (Col. 3:1). Why is Christ seated there—what is the necessary implication of that seated position? It is not because He is the head of His church; this is not Paul's point here (although he made *that* point in Col. 1:18). It is because Christ is the King, and anyone who wants Christ to save him must "keep seeking" His kingdom's teachings, virtues, concerns, and servitude. Again, this is not church talk; this is kingdom talk.

Love and Service: Another way to support the kingdom is to love and serve one another. While it is true that church members (Christians) should be loving and serving people, the emphasis of this teaching is not about what goes on in a church context but what citizens of the kingdom do in response to the character and conduct of their King.

"A new commandment I give to you, that you love one another, even as I have loved you, that you also love one another," Jesus taught. "By this all men will know that you are My disciples, if you have love for one another" (John 13:34–35). The "one another" phrase virtually always has reference to fellow Christians in the NT. However, this is not a teaching about what we do because we are members of His church but because we are imitators of our Master, the King.

Serving one another is likewise not church work, since the church is not the servant, but members *of* the church are servants. Jesus never told the church to go serve one another but He did tell His kingdom citizens that servitude is the route to greatness *in the kingdom* (see Mat. 20:20–28, where the conversation is not about who sits where regarding the church but the kingdom of God). Too many Christians think that the church is to serve, and their role is only to attend the church's services and maybe put money in the church's collection plate. But genuine servitude is the lifestyle of kingdom citizens, not churchgoers.

"You call Me Teacher and Lord; and you are right, for so I am," Jesus told His disciples. "If I then, the Lord and the Teacher, washed your feet, you also ought to wash one another's feet. For I gave you an example that you also should do as I did to you" (John 13:13–15). This instruction is not about church protocol or what is to be done amid a church service.

When Jesus identifies Himself as "Lord," He refers to His kingly role, not His head-of-the-church role. He is never called the Lord of His church; but, as King over God's kingdom, He most certainly is Lord over all that has come into existence. And in this role, He instructs His citizens to follow His servant-hearted example.

Think about what Peter wrote: "Therefore, brethren, be all the more diligent to make certain about His calling and choosing you; for as long as you practice these things, you will never stumble; for in this way the entrance into the eternal kingdom of our Lord and Savior Jesus Christ will be abundantly supplied to you" (2 Peter 1:10–11). He does not mention the church here because the Christians to whom he wrote were already members of the church in real time. However, they had *yet* to inherit the eternal kingdom of God as it will be fully revealed in the hereafter. God will abundantly supply the means of this inheritance (i.e., the full realization of our "entrance"), but only if one proves diligent to live like a kingdom citizen.

Summary Thoughts: Christians often define what they do for the brotherhood as "church work"—maybe not with those words but certainly with that understanding. But it is helpful for us to see every brother or sister in Christ (i.e., as a member of His church) as a citizen of His kingdom. It is good for Christian husbands to regard their Christian wives, for example, as citizens of the kingdom and not only like-minded believers. When Peter tells husbands to treat their wives as "fellow heirs" (1 Peter 3:7), he is using kingdom talk, not church talk. Christians are not heirs of the church, but, if we are faithful, we will inherit the kingdom.

Whatever Christians do to support God's kingdom also support Christ's church. In fact, it cannot be otherwise. (The opposite is also true: when we work against the kingdom, we also work against the church.) There are different ways to support the kingdom. My examples have included: support Christ's authority, both in your own life and as you share the gospel *of* the kingdom with others. Support the virtues of the kingdom, both in your own conduct as well as promoting them as fitting for all people. And practice the love and servitude that the King, in His earthly ministry, showed to the world.

If you are a member of Christ's church, then you have obeyed what the gospel of Christ requires for this. It cannot be otherwise. And if you are a member of Christ's church, you are also a citizen of God's kingdom, even though the full realization of this citizenship is offered to you in promise and is not yet a finished conclusion. Remain faithful until your life is over and Christ will honor you with a crown of life (Rev. 2:10).

The crown of life is not about church membership, and Christ putting it on your head is not because He is the head of His church. It is about kingdom citizenship, and He *as* the King has the right to induct you into the heavenly and eternal kingdom in the life to come. And "it is for this that we labor and strive, because we have fixed our hope on the living God" (1 Tim. 4:10).

Chapter Fifteen

Inheriting the Kingdom of God

An inheritance is usually a good thing. If you have ever inherited something from your parents (or a kind benefactor), likely it was something of importance, value, and benefit to you. This is how it should be in the human realm, and this is how it is regarding the realm to come.

To inherit the kingdom is to inherit eternal life. These are not two separate things but the same. If one inherits the kingdom, he inherits eternal life; and vice versa. Just as the Holy Spirit cannot be separated from the Father, so an heir of the kingdom cannot be separated from the life that that inheritance provides.

No one will inherit God's kingdom who is evil, immoral, idolatrous, or unbelieving. The NT is clear and unapologetic on this. Those who seek the kingdom wrongly—say, by force (Luke 16:16), self-justification, or failure to serve God's people (Mat. 25:41–45)—will not be its heirs. The King determines the conditions of this entrance, not people, preachers, churches, or religions. We should strive to honor the King and His requests, not look for shortcuts, loopholes, or customized alterations to them.

Our Future Resurrection: Seeking the kingdom of God and His righteousness looks beyond this world and into the world to come. We are not only seeking what is here, but what is there; not only what is now, but what will be; and not only what we *are* now, but what we *will* be. This takes us to the resurrection—not Jesus' but our own. Jesus was the "first fruits" of the resurrection of the righteous (1 Cor. 15:20); ours follows His, both in sequence and in form. As He was resurrected, so we will be. We are seeking a future resurrection from the dead even while we are now very much alive.

Christianity is not the origin of resurrection beliefs. The Jews believed in a national resurrection of all righteous Israelites, thus seeing themselves in a glorified picture with their Messiah. Their belief in His resurrection from the dead was the culmination of that role. This is what Martha referred to in her discussion with Jesus in Bethany concerning her brother Lazarus (John 11:23–24). "The pious Israelite being certain, that his personal and indeed his enduring and eternal salvation is the will of God, expects that he and all the godly will have a share in the future glory of the nation. He then who is seized by death before this is realized, may hope that he will one day be raised up again by God and transplanted to the kingdom of His glory."[109]

Jesus went on to tell Martha that He Himself was "the resurrection and the life" (John 11:25). As King of God's kingdom, He would experience a human death but could not be constrained by it. As Peter later said, "God raised Him up again, putting an end to the agony of death, since it was impossible for Him to be held in its power" (Acts 2:24). The King who overcame death will also, on our behalf, overcome our physical death as well. As He was resurrected bodily, so will we; as He came out of His own grave, so He will bring us out of ours (John 5:28–29).

"Now I say this, brethren, that flesh and blood cannot inherit the kingdom of God; nor does the perishable inherit the imperishable" (1 Cor. 15:50). This applies in both senses: presently, as in embracing God's rule over one's earthly life; and in a future sense, when all those who have done the first thing will be glorified in the hereafter. For now, we partake of this first sense; for the second and future experience, Christ must bring our bodies back to life and then transform them for a heavenly existence (1 Cor. 15:51–53).

This subject involves details we do not know or cannot understand. We know we will be changed from a physical being to a purely spiritual one. This spiritual transformation will not leave us bodiless, however; we will simply have a different kind of body. We know Christ will transform us into a glorious being that reflects His own glory (Phil. 3:20–21, 1 John

3:2, etc.). Beyond this, there are many things we do not know, nor do we need to know them.

But just because we do not have all the answers does not undermine or nullify the predicted event of our future resurrection. The purpose of our resurrection is to bring us to completion—body, soul, and spirit (1 Thess. 5:23)—so that we can enter the heavenly kingdom as we were fully meant to be: in God's image. But though the different manifestations of our existence must be reunited, so to speak, in this way, we cannot enter the kingdom in glory while still in the form of the old Creation. We must be transformed on the ascent of our resurrected body on earth to heavenly glory (1 Cor. 15:40–49, 1 Thess. 4:13–17).

"And so we shall always be with the Lord." Our resurrection is not the end of our existence but merely a transition to our eternal one. Death ends the earthly experience of our seeking the kingdom and God's righteousness. But our resurrection is the entrance *into* that heavenly kingdom and the personal and visible realization *of* that righteousness. We will then no longer be seekers since what we had been seeking in this life will be ours in the life to come. As God has opened to us the doors to His kingdom, so we will, because of His mercy and grace, inherit that kingdom.

The Form of Our Inheritance: This begs the question that we have not yet addressed directly: What does it mean to "inherit the kingdom"? The phrase is used repeatedly in the NT, both positively (as to what will be given) and negatively (as to what will be denied).[110] Similarly, the NT speaks of faithful believers in Christ as "heirs," which is why the term "sons" is often used rather than "children" (Gal. 3:26–27). In the ancient world, sons were the expected heirs of their fathers' estates; daughters usually were not.[111] "Therefore you are no longer a slave [of sin], but a son [of God]; and if a son, then an heir through God" (Gal. 4:7, bracketed words added).

We know Christ is the appointed "heir of all things" (Heb. 1:2), and that He Himself has said, "All things that the Father has are Mine" (John

16:15). But Christ did not die for the kingdom; He did not purchase it with His blood, as He did the church. His Father rightfully and legally transferred His kingdom to His Son as an inheritance, to execute the kingdom's work in the Father's name. Thus, Christ inherited His Father's kingdom, and within that kingdom He built His church in His Father's name (as a church of God).

If Christ is the heir of all things, what then is there for us to inherit? The answer is that we inherit all things *through* Him. As Paul wrote: "The Spirit Himself testifies with our spirit that we are children of God, and if children, heirs also, heirs of God and fellow heirs with Christ, if indeed we suffer with Him so that we may also be glorified with Him" (Rom. 8:16–17). We are "fellow heirs with Christ," so that we are sharers in all that the Father has given to Him. To "inherit the kingdom," then, is not an inheritance apart from Christ's own inheritance but unites the two things together.

The kingdom of God is (from Acts 2 forward) often described as something we *will* enter, as describing a future event. We *have* entered it through our faith and God's promise, but we have not yet proven ourselves to be faithful until death (Rev. 2:10). Christ *did* prove Himself faithful until death, but He did so perfectly, not through trial and error as we do.

Thus, our sonship is based upon an adoption into God's spiritual family, the church. And our inheritance is based on what Christ has accomplished, not what we have accomplished. We are heirs based on His merit, not our own. Everything God does for us that we cannot do ourselves is an act of grace, and most certainly He makes us heirs of the kingdom through His grace and not through our personal performance. The only thing we contribute is our faith in God, His Son, and His grace.

What will this look like, to inherit the kingdom in the life to come? No one can say with certainty of its details, but "We know that when He appears, we will be like Him, because we will see Him just as He is" (1 John 3:2). This not only refers to how we see Him in His Second

Coming, but also how we will *be* with Him in eternity. We will not merely see the King; we will be with Him forever. We will enjoy all the virtues and attributes of God's kingdom that Christ disclosed to us in His ministry. "Your eyes will see the King in His beauty" (Isa. 33:17)—the prophet Isaiah here is referring to the Jews seeing Jesus, both in person and in faith. However, this thought can also apply to what we all will see in heaven—no longer in faith but in fact.

Christ does give us glimpses of this inheritance, or at least the blessings of this inheritance, in His letters to the seven churches of Asia in Rev. 2 – 3. Think about what He says to "him who overcomes":

- "I will grant to eat of the tree of life which is in the Paradise of God" (Rev. 2:7). This "tree of life" implies immortality, just as it did in the original Garden of Eden (Gen. 3:22). Those who inherit God's kingdom will live forever; they will never die.[112]
- "will not be hurt by the second death" (Rev. 2:11). The first death is one's human or physical death; the second death is hell, "the lake of fire" (Rev. 20:14). Those who inherit God's kingdom will never need to fear or face hell (separation and punishment) again.
- "to him I will give some of the hidden manna, and I will give him a white stone, and a new name written on the stone which no one knows but he who receives it" (Rev. 2:17). The power to name someone shows a higher rank or authority than the one who is named (as in Gen. 2:19–20, 23). Those who inherit God's kingdom will receive a new name from Christ Himself. We will not merely extend or resume our earthly identity in the life to come; we will be given a new identity, one that is so sacred and intimate that no one knows it but Christ and the recipient of that name.
- "to him I will give authority over the nations; and he shall rule them with a rod of iron, as the vessels of the potter are broken to pieces, as I also have received authority from My Father; and I will give him the morning star" (2:26–28).
  - I confess that I do not fully understand all of what Christ is saying here, but there are some things that can be known. God will give those who inherit His kingdom the authority to judge

those who defy God. This alludes to what Paul said: "Or do you not know that the saints will judge the world? ... Do you not know that we will judge angels?" (1 Cor. 6:2–3; compare Mat. 19:28, in principle). God's heirs will "judge the world" in the sense that we have proven our faithfulness to the King and thus represent Him in *His* judgment of the world. If broken people can choose an invisible God over what caused their brokenness, should not angels in His presence choose to remain loyal to Him?
- The "morning star" (which, literally, is the planet Venus) figuratively implies a brilliant light that comes through the darkness, just as Venus appears as the night disappears and a new day is dawning. This describes God's people in glory: they have come through the darkness of this world and now shine as lights in the cosmos (compare Phil. 2:15).

❑ "will thus be clothed in white garments; and I will not erase his name from the book of life, and I will confess his name before My Father and before His angels" (Rev. 3:5). White garments signify purity and innocence; those who inherit the kingdom of God will have been purified of their sins and guilt through the blood of Christ (Col. 1:19–22). Their names will be in the "book of life," which is God's record (i.e., roster of citizenry) of those who belong to Him (Luke 10:20, Rev. 20:12). Christ will personally vouch for these people before His Father that they *were* faithful to Him and that He *does* identify them as His own (compare Mat. 7:21–23).

❑ "I will make him a pillar in the temple of My God, and he will not go out from it anymore; and I will write on him the name of My God, and the name of the city of My God, the new Jerusalem, which comes down out of heaven from My God, and My new name" (Rev. 3:12). Having God's and Christ's name written on you means that you belong to them and are their possession forever (compare Exod. 21:5–6, in principle). The "city" and "new Jerusalem" refer to Christ's church; all who belong to Christ also belong to His church. His church will be brought into heaven as a collective body of souls. Those who inherit the kingdom of God will forever identify with God and with all others who identify with Him.

- ❏ "I will grant to him to sit down with Me on My throne, as I also overcame and sat down with My Father on His throne" (Rev. 3:21). This does not merely refer to authority (although this too, as we saw in 2:26–28) but also glory, privilege, and incalculable esteem. To sit down next to the Father is the highest honor that any soul could ever hope to enjoy—a higher honor than offered to any angel (Heb. 1:13). This will prove as greatly as ever could be proved that we belong to God and are His forever. Those who inherit the kingdom of God will be highly exalted, just as Christ was (Phil. 2:9) and God promised to do (1 Peter 5:6).

There are many glories that come with inheriting the kingdom of God. Some of these we know and can anticipate; others will exist that we do not know but that will be wonderful beyond human imagination, to be sure. Heirs will be, after all, enjoying the splendor and majesty of the highest power that exists. In such a context, no one will ever be disappointed.

To Those Who Overcome: One final question remains: what does it mean to "overcome"? We know that Jesus overcame the world (and sin, death, and Satan) (John 16:33). But in His "to him who overcomes" statements to the seven churches He does not talk about what He did but what we must do *for* Him, *with* Him, and *through* Him. We overcome not on our own power or resourcefulness but by relying on His power, strength, and grace. We overcome this world not because *we* are more powerful than it but because *He* is, and we put our confidence and trust in His power.

In overcoming the world, we also overcome what "the world" represents: sin, death, and Satan. We are not capable of overcoming any of these on our own, but Christ is—and He proved it through His resurrection from the dead. When we are baptized by that same authority by which He overcame the world, we align ourselves with the King and thus He will save us, if we remain faithful to Him (1 Peter 3:21–22).

To "overcome the world" sounds very general, however. Perhaps we should look at it this way as well: we need to overcome *our* world—I need to overcome mine, and you need to overcome yours. By this is meant the sphere of people, activity, and lifestyle with which you interact throughout your life.

Within this sphere, you will encounter false people, false teachers, and false doctrines: you must overcome these with Christ and His truth. You will encounter illicit desires, temptations to sin, and stumbling blocks: you must overcome these by taking the "way of escape" (1 Cor. 10:13). You will encounter trials, adversities, and storms of life: you must overcome these by letting Christ lead you through them. You will encounter trials and threats to your faith: you must overcome these by clinging even more tightly to the Savior and His word.

Heirs of the kingdom of God are overcomers, not underachievers. They are victors, not victims; succeeders, not failures; warriors, not deserters. They persevere in faith, not give up in unbelief. They are faithful husbands and wives, edifying mentors and teachers, diligent deacons, bold preachers, and wise shepherds. They are men and women who remain "faithful until death" (Rev. 2:10) to the King and His kingdom. They may fall from time to time; they may face great spiritual crises and even moral failures, but they get back up and continue walking the narrow way that leads to life.

To inherit the kingdom of God is, in part, to realize that this world is not your home. This realization must translate to your sincere and responsible course of action toward the King and His eternal kingdom.

Summary Thoughts: Believers seek God's kingdom, and thus seek God's appointed King, not only for the sake of this life but also the life to come. As God resurrected the King from the dead, never to die again but to live forever, so He will resurrect the King's people to eternal life. We can be confident of this because the King has promised it, and His word cannot fail. Our resurrection is the transition between what we sought on earth and what we receive in heaven. "[T]he eternal kingdom of our Lord and Savior Jesus Christ will be abundantly supplied" in the hereafter to those who lived according to its character, values, and moral purity in the here-and-now (2 Peter 1:11).

Those who inherit the kingdom of God are those who overcome this present world through their faith in Christ the King. They are those who set their mind on Him and His kingdom rather than on any other lord or kingdom. Christ has promised many wonderful rewards to those who walk in love, light, and truth. He will not bend the rules to accommodate passive believers; He will not admit anyone into the eternal kingdom who is ruled by doubt, fear, or unbelief.

However, His grace will overcome every deficiency, inadequacy, or failure that we experience in our human state of being. Whatever we cannot do but must be done, He will do it. Whatever we lack because of our human frailty and limitations, He will compensate with mercy and grace. As God promised, "I will be merciful to their iniquities, and I will remember their sins no more" (Heb. 8:12).

If we remain faithful to the King, one day we will see Him in His glory. We will see the beauty of His kingdom. We will be *heirs* of that kingdom forever. This is His promise to us—to you.

Sources Used for
The Kingdom of God: A Biblical Perspective

Barnes, Albert. *Barnes' Notes on the New Testament* (electronic edition). Database © 2014 by WORDsearch Corp.

Bright, John. *The Kingdom of God.* Nashville, TN: Abingdon Press, 1981.

Clarke, Adam. *Adam Clarke's Commentary* (electronic edition). Database © 2014 by WORDsearch Corp.

Edersheim, Alfred. *The Life and Times of Jesus the Messiah.* Peabody, MA: Hendrickson Publishers, 1993.

Hendriksen, William. *New Testament Commentary: Matthew.* Grand Rapids: Baker Book House, 1973.

Holman Bible Dictionary (electronic edition). © 1991 by Holman Bible Publishers; database © 2008 by WORDsearch Corp.

International Standard Bible Encyclopedia (electronic edition). © 1979 by Eerdman's Publishing Co.; database © 2013 by WORDsearch Corp.

Jamieson, Robert, A. R. Fausset, and David Brown. *Commentary Critical and Explanatory on the Whole Bible, 1871* (electronic edition). Database © 2012 by WORDsearch Corp.

Josephus. *Josephus Complete Works.* Trans. by William Whiston. Grand Rapids: Kregel Publications, 1978.

Ladd, George Eldon. *The Gospel of the Kingdom: Scriptural Studies in the Kingdom of God.* Grand Rapids: Eerdmans Publishing Co., 1990; orig., Paternoster Press, 1959.

Lenski, R. C. H. *The Interpretation of St. Matthew's Gospel.* Peabody, MA: Hendrickson Publishers, 1998.

Lloyd-Jones, Martyn. *The Kingdom of God.* Wheaton, IL: Crossway, 1992.

McGuiggan, Jim. *The Reign of God.* Fort Worth, TX: Star Bible Publications, 1992.

Mitchell, Paul. (Unpublished comments.)

Perrin, Nicholas. *The Kingdom of God: A Biblical Theology.* Grand Rapids: Zondervan, 2019.

Ridderbos, Herman N. *The Coming of the Kingdom.* Trans. by H. de Jongste. Philadelphia: The Presbyterian and Reformed Publishing Co., 1962.

Shurer, Emil. *A History of the Jewish People in the Time of Christ.* Trans. by John MacPherson. Peabody, MA: Hendrickson Publishers, 1995; orig., Edinburgh: T & T Clark, 1890.

Strong, James. *Strong's Talking Greek-Hebrew Dictionary.* Database © WORDsearch Corp.

Sychtysz, Chad. *The Gospel of Saving Grace.* Waynesville, OH: Spiritbuilding Publishers, 2020.

_____. *The New Testament Pattern: God's Plan for Christians and Their Churches* (Waynesville, OH: Spiritbuilding Publishers, 2023.

_____. *This World Is Not Your Home.* Waynesville, OH: Spiritbuilding Publishers, 2021.

_____. *Seeking the Sacred.* Waynesville, OH: Spiritbuilding Publishers, 2009.

Thayer, Joseph. *Thayer's Greek-English Lexicon* (electronic edition). Database © 2014 by WORDsearch Corp.

The Zondervan Pictorial Encyclopedia of the Bible, vol. 3; Merrill. C. Tenney, gen. ed. Grand Rapids: Regency Reference Library, 1976.

Vincent, Martin R. *Vincent's Word Studies in the New Testament* (electronic edition). Database © 2014 by WORDsearch Corp.

Wharton, Edward C. *The Church of Christ: The Distinctive Nature of the New Testament Church.* Nashville, TN: The Gospel Advocate Co., 1997.

Endnotes

1   This is evident in John 8:33, when they proudly told Jesus, "We are Abraham's descendants and have never yet been enslaved to anyone; how is it that You say, 'You will become free'?" However, when it was politically expedient to do so, they feigned allegiance to Roman authority, as seen in John 19:15, when they just as proudly proclaimed, "We have no king but Caesar."

2   This is not the same Theudas of which Josephus spoke ("Antiquities," 20.5.1, *Josephus Complete Works*, trans. by William Whiston [Grand Rapids: Kregel Publications, 1978]), but a man with the same name some twelve years after him (Robert Jamieson, A. R. Fausset, and David Brown, *Commentary Critical and Explanatory on the Whole Bible, 1871*, electronic edition [database © 2012 by WORDsearch Corp.], on Acts 5:36).

3   Josephus, "Antiquities," 13.1.1.

4   Emil Shurer, *A History of the Jewish People in the Time of Christ*, trans. by John MacPherson (Peabody, MA: Hendrickson Publishers, 1995; orig., Edinburgh: T & T Clark, 1890), 2nd div., 2:129–131.

5   According to modern Jews: "Foreign nations would not be obliterated in the messianic era. Nations such as Rome would come to the Messiah to pay tribute to him, but their appeals for favor would be rejected [BT Pesahim 118b] ... Still others held that humans would take on a new appearance: some thought that man would achieve a height of 160 feet, while another suggested he might double that. There is no suggestion that the Messiah himself is a wonder worker, but many sages believed that the messianic age would be a time of wonders. Women would give birth painlessly, hens lay eggs continuously, and food appear in abundance [BT Shabbat 30b]" (cited from https://www.myjewishlearning.com/article/the-messianic-age-in-judaism/).

6   George Eldon Ladd, *The Gospel of the Kingdom: Scriptural Studies in the Kingdom of God* (Grand Rapids: Eerdmans Publishing Co., 1990 [orig. Paternoster Press, 1959]), 100.

7   In my opinion, many today who identify as Christians are what might be better identified as "religious moralists"—people who go to church and hold to a righteous standard of living, but do not abide by the entirety of the NT pattern for Christians and their churches. While Christians must be, in fact, morally pure, morality by itself is not a method of salvation. No one can be made morally pure apart from the blood of Christ, and no one can receive the blood of Christ without being faithful to all that Christ and His apostles have instructed.

8   Nicholas Perrin, *The Kingdom of God: A Biblical Theology* (Grand Rapids: Zondervan, 2019), 52; bracketed words are mine; emphasis is his.

9   To clarify, I will use "God" throughout this book to refer to God the Father, the head of the triune Godhead of the Father, Son, and Holy Spirit, unless otherwise noted.

10   See also Isa. 45:5–7, 18, 21–22, and 46:9.

11   See also Exod. 8:10, Isa. 43:10, 45:5–7, and Joel 2:27.

12   This is evident in John 1:1–3, 10, 1 Cor. 8:6, Col. 1:16, and Heb. 1:2. Divine Beings (the Father, Son, and Holy Spirit) are uncreated Beings; they have always existed and have no beginning point in time. All else—the physical world, the spiritual world, angels, and human beings—have a point in time when they began to exist (or, were brought into existence). In Rev. 4:11 and 10:6, it says that God the Father is the Creator, but this simply credits Him as the source of all creative power. It is like saying that Moses built the tabernacle of God (when he did not literally do so) or Solomon built the temple of God in Jerusalem (when he did not), when in fact these men were the source of authority *for* these creations. God the *Son* "built" the Creation, so to speak, but He did so by His Father's authority and not as a unilateral or independent action.

13   This is a point I make in my book *Seeking the Sacred* (Spiritbuilding Publishers, 2009; go to www.spiritbuilding.com/chad), 54–74.

14   C. H. Dodd, quoted in Jim McGuiggan, *The Reign of God* (Fort Worth, TX: Star Bible Publications, 1992), 18; bracketed words are mine.

15 Ladd, *The Gospel of the Kingdom*, 19.

16 Moses predicted that this would happen; see Deut. 17:14–15. By "unformed," I mean a god that was not represented by a human-made image. In fact, God explicitly forbade this (Exod. 20:3–4).

17 McGuiggan, 24.

18 Alfred Edersheim, *The Life and Times of Jesus the Messiah* (Peabody, MA: Hendrickson Publishers, 1993), 187.

19 McGuiggan, 57.

20 This is what Paul means in Rom. 3:23–25. All have sinned, therefore all need to be saved. This salvation (or "justification" in legal terminology) is made possible through Christ's "propitiation" (i.e., satisfaction or appeasement of God's wrath toward sin), His blood sacrifice on the cross. This propitiation extends to those who preceded this offering in time ("the sins previously committed") as well as those committed after it.

21 "A name is an icon, a flag, a standard, a symbol that represents the power and ethic of a nation or person. The Babelites [*sic*] were rejecting all these symbols of God's kingdom for their own self-rule" (Paul Mitchell).

22 Jesse, a descendant of the union of Boaz and Ruth, was David's father (Ruth 4:17). Jesse had seven other sons, making David the eighth son (1 Sam. 16:1–13), the number eight in Scripture indicating a new power, strength, life, dynasty, or beginning.

23 A "mystery" in Scripture is "a truth that is hidden from the natural man," and "is something that he has to be shown" by God (Martyn Lloyd-Jones, *The Kingdom of God* [Wheaton, IL: Crossway, 1992], 92). The "pride of intellect"—an overconfidence in one's own knowledge and understanding, as though it were superior to what God reveals to him—is the greatest hindrance to understanding God's "mystery" of His kingdom (*Ibid.*, 94); such pride creates mental and intellectual prejudice, which dismisses any fact or evidence that disagrees with one's own conclusion, despite the worthiness, credibility, and truthfulness of such proofs.

24   "Propitiation" is a satisfaction or appeasement of something. In this case, Christ's blood is the appeasement of God's wrath toward the sinner to whom that blood is applied (Rom. 5:6–10).

25   George E. Ladd, "Kingdom of God," *International Standard Bible Encyclopedia*, electronic edition (© 1979 by Eerdman's Publishing Co.; database © 2013 by WORDsearch Corp.); bracketed words are mine.

26   Edersheim, 183–184.

27   Joseph Thayer, *Thayer's Greek–English Lexicon*, electronic edition (database © 2014 by WORDsearch Corp.); G3772, bracketed words are mine.

28   Marvin R. Vincent, *Vincent's Word Studies in the New Testament*, electronic edition (database © 2014 by WORDsearch Corp.), on Mat. 3:2.

29   Ladd, "Kingdom of God," *ISBE*; bracketed words are mine. "Jesus spoke Aramaic; the Gospel writers translated Jesus' sermons and parables into Greek. Mark, Luke, and John translated Jesus' words as 'kingdom of God.' Matthew sometimes used this phrase too, but often he preferred to translate Jesus' Aramaic words as 'kingdom of heaven.' The two phrases mean exactly the same thing, because they are translations of the same Aramaic words of Jesus" (Fisher Humphreys, "kingdom of God," *Holman Bible Dictionary*, electronic edition [© 1991 by Holman Bible Publishers; database © 2008 by WORDsearch Corp.]). "According to Rabbinic views of the time [i.e., in Jesus' day], the terms 'Kingdom,' 'Kingdom of heaven,' and 'Kingdom of God'… were equivalent. In fact, the word 'heaven' was very often used instead of 'God,' so as to avoid unduly familiarizing the ear with the Sacred Name. This, probably, accounts for the exclusive use of the expression 'Kingdom of Heaven' in the Gospel by St. Matthew" (Edersheim, 184–5).

30   William Hendriksen, *New Testament Commentary: Matthew* (Grand Rapids: Baker Book House, 1973), 249; emphases are all his.

31   Shurer, 2nd div., 2:171. A metonym is a literary device in which one thing represents a thing to which it belongs, as when we say Washington (the physical U.S. capital) to represent the entire U.S. government.

32   McGuiggan, 64.

33   *Ibid.*, 11.

34   *Ibid.*, 64.

35   Edersheim, 403.

36   Calvinism places this responsibility solely on God: "By predestination we mean the eternal decree of God, by which he determined with himself whatever he wished to happen with regard to every man. All are not created on equal terms, but some are preordained to eternal life, others to eternal damnation; and, accordingly, as each has been created for one or other of these ends, we say that he has been predestinated to life or to death" (John Calvin, *Institutes of the Christian Religion*, book 3, chapter 21, section 5, electronic edition [database © 2007 by WORDsearch Corp.]). This is not a biblical teaching. I discuss Calvinism and its inherent flaws in my book, *The Gospel of Saving Grace*, chapter 17; go to www.spiritbuilding.com/chad.

37   Herman N. Ridderbos, *The Coming of the Kingdom*, trans. by H. de Jongste (Philadelphia: The Presbyterian and Reformed Publishing Co., 1962), 125.

38   Ladd, *The Gospel of the Kingdom*, 53.

39   "The Messiah and His history are not presented in the Old Testament as something separate from, or superadded to, Israel. The history, the institutions, and the predictions of Israel run up into Him. … He is the Son of God and the Servant of the Lord… As He was 'anointed' to be the 'Servant of the Lord,' not with the typical oil, but by 'the Spirit of Jehovah' upon Him, so was He also the 'Son' in a unique sense. … Moreover, the Messiah, as Representative Israelite, combined in Himself as 'the Servant of the Lord' the threefold office of Prophet, Priest, and King, and joined together the two ideas of 'Son' and 'Servant' (Phil. 2:6–11). And the final combination and full exhibition of these two ideas was the fulfillment of the typical mission of Israel, and the establishment of the Kingdom of God among men" (Edersheim, 114).

40   "Judaism" requires adherence to the Law of Moses, circumcision of men, and observance of rabbinic traditions. In Acts 15:1, 5, some Jewish Christians insisted that Gentile believers to "observe the Law of Moses"

as well as their commitment to Christ. This was rejected by both the Holy Spirit and the apostles, and Paul later spoke out against this directly and forcefully (see Gal. 5:1–6, for example).

41   The Jews likely saw Isa. 53, for example (which directly anticipates this suffering), as a symbolic depiction of the nation of Israel and not as Israel's Messiah. The nation would suffer for the sake of righteousness; the nation would be praised by God for its piety; etc. Thus, Israel saw their entire nation as a martyr for God rather than a single person (compare Acts 8:29–35, where Philip directly links Jesus to Isa. 53).

42   This perspective did not include persecution for one's faith, which the Jews themselves had endured for centuries by the time Jesus entered the picture. Indeed, Jesus died as the recipient of religious and political persecution, not because of crimes He had committed. He was the world's most genuine martyr.

43   I. H. Marshall, "kingdom of God" *The Zondervan Pictorial Encyclopedia of the Bible*, vol. 3; Merrill. C. Tenney, gen. ed. (Grand Rapids: Regency Reference Library, 1976), 804.

44   This is especially true since Jesus' riding on a donkey into Jerusalem was the fulfillment of OT Scripture (Zech. 9:9), of which the Jews and Jewish rulers ought to have been quite familiar.

45   A "centurion" originally was a Roman military commander of one hundred (L., *centurio*, "century") of men. Later, the number of men under his command varied, but the rank name was still used.

46   James Strong, *Strong's Talking Greek–Hebrew Dictionary*, electronic edition (database © WORDsearch Corp.) and Thayer (electronic), G3439.

47   The Greek word for "appointed" here is far more often translated "laid [down]," "put," or "made" (Strong, G5087).

48   This is similar to when Paul calls Christ's gospel "my gospel"—one that he (Paul) preaches by Christ's authority—even though he does not own this gospel (Rom. 2:16). See also Rom. 16:25, 1 Cor. 15:1, Gal. 1:11, and 2 Tim. 2:8.

49   Strong, H4428 and H6664. See Heb. 7:2, where he is identified as "king of righteousness" by name but "king of Salem [peace]" according to his position.

50   Ridderbos, 82; bracketed words are mine.

51   I have written in far greater detail information about the church in my book, *The New Testament Pattern: God's Plan for Christians and Their Churches* (Spiritbuilding Publishers, 2021); go to www.spiritbuilding.com/chad.

52   Acts 20:28, 1 Cor. 10:32, 11:22, 15:9, Gal. 1:13, and 1 Tim. 3:15.

53   1 Cor. 1:2, 2 Cor. 1:1, 1 Thess. 1:1, and 2 Thess. 1:1.

54   In Col 1:15–18, Christ's supremacy over all things created is stated directly, without reference to His having been "given" or "appointed" anything by His Father. The two passages (Eph. 1:19–22 and Col. 1:18) should be taken together; the one explains the other.

55   Mat. 4:23, 9:35, 24:14, and Luke 16:16.

56   Hendriksen, 250; bracketed words are mine.

57   McGuiggan, 29.

58   This requires, of course, that a person be a sinner to be saved from his sins. One who has never sinned—i.e., an innocent child—does not need to be saved because he has nothing for which to be atoned. Christians should never try to rescue those who are not yet lost.

59   This is what I understand Paul to be saying in Rom. 8:19–23.

60   Hendriksen, 250; bracketed words are mine.

61   There are many Christians today who believe that Jesus changed the Law of Moses and made a few laws of His own prior to His crucifixion. This is not true; in fact, it cannot be true. If Jesus changed any laws which God gave to His people, then He would be a lawbreaker and not a law-keeper. He could not be justified by a Law that He failed to keep, in which case He could not be our Savior.

62   To be the "least" in this context—in reference to one's standing before God—really means to be exempted from any honorable standing in the kingdom, which is to be alienated from the kingdom altogether. "He who, by his mode of acting, speaking, or explaining the words of God, sets the holy precept aside, or explains away its force and meaning, shall be called least—shall have no place in the kingdom of Christ here, nor in the kingdom of glory above. That this is the meaning of these words [in Mat. 5:19] is evident enough from the following verse [Mat.

5:20]" (Adam Clarke, *Adam Clarke's Commentary*, electronic edition [database © 2014 by WORDsearch Corp.], on Mat. 5:19). Compare 1 Sam. 2:30, where "lightly esteemed" really means no esteem at all. Such contrastive language is poeticized for effect.

63 Strong, G4318.

64 Humphreys, *Holman* (electronic).

65 Ladd, *The Gospel of the Kingdom*, 137.

66 For further study on "grace," I strongly recommend my book, *The Gospel of Saving Grace* (Spiritbuilding Publishers, 2020); go to www.spiritbuilding.com/chad.

67 Thayer, G932.

68 Edward C. Wharton, *The Church of Christ: The Distinctive Nature of the New Testament Church* (Nashville, TN: The Gospel Advocate Co., 1997), 56; bracketed words are added; emphasis is mine.

69 Ladd, "Kingdom of God," *ISBE* (electronic).

70 Thayer, G932.

71 McGuiggan, 59; bracketed citation is mine.

72 Ladd, *The Gospel of the Kingdom*, 63.

73 *Ibid.*, 31; bracketed words are mine.

74 *Ibid.*, 34.

75 JFB, on Mat. 6:10.

76 R. C. H. Lenski, *The Interpretation of St. Matthew's Gospel* (Peabody, MA: Hendrickson Publishers, 1998), 94.

77 We should think of the church (as a corporate entity) as being part of God's eternal kingdom but not the entirety of it. Christ does not reign only over the church; He reigns over all the angels as well, and whatever dominions or principalities that they manage. So, the church and the kingdom, even in the future context, are not the same thing: one (the church) will become part of the other (the kingdom), not the other way around. The church will "inherit" the kingdom in that it will become part of it forever.

78 A system of sin → repentance → begging pardon → forgiveness is all we know. But this is only for the here and now. Grace, forgiveness,

blood atonement, etc. are all part of God's covenant relationship with us. The only reason for a covenant is to deal with sin. In the absence of sin, there is no need for a mediation between the sinner and the One sinned against. God did not have a covenant with Adam and Eve in the beginning; only after they sinned do we see indication of a covenant (however simple or primitive it might have been), as signified by the offering of animals for blood atonement [implied]. But prior to their having sinned, God only had law, and if they kept that law, they were justified by their own innocence. We (on earth) are in a context in which we have not seen God, and (for us) have not seen with our own eyes the source of our atonement (Christ and His crucifixion). So, we live by faith, not by sight (2 Cor. 5:7), and God in His love and mercy gives us opportunity to seek rectification of our mistakes. (Angels do not have this opportunity because they already see God; compare Mat. 18:10, Heb. 2:16, and 2 Peter 2:4.) Once we see God, we will no longer live by faith; we will also no longer need to have a covenant relationship with God, because all covenants between God and people are fulfilled in Christ, and we will be with Christ by then, and all will have been completed, fulfilled, satisfied, etc. through Him. Once we have been made innocent by Christ's blood to be in the eternal kingdom, we will be forever "changed" to accommodate that new life (1 Cor. 15:50ff, Phil. 3:20–21, 1 John 3:2, etc.). We will not need a new covenant; there is zero mention of a "newer" covenant in the life to come. There is no Scripture that directly says we cannot sin in heaven; there is also no Scripture that says we can or will. God does promise that in the glorious afterlife there will be no more sorrow, pain, or suffering—all the consequences of sin: "and He will wipe away every tear from their eyes; and there will no longer be any death; there will no longer be any mourning, or crying, or pain; the first things have passed away" (Rev. 21:4). If there are no consequences of sin in heaven, then it stands to reason that there will be no sin to cause those consequences. The "first things" include all temptations we have had to endure while choosing to follow Christ rather than anything else; once the test is completed, there will be victory, not yet another test (James 1:12). We will have already run the race, etc.—there will not be another one to run in which we can fail, fall short, etc. (2 Tim. 4:7–8). We will not be only temporarily triumphant but eternally so: God has promised this. Implied in all this is the idea that we, already having been tested, will in heaven know perfectly what it was that once tested us, and we will have mastered that situation. This is why, I believe, we will be able to judge angels who have sinned, because we will have endured something that they have never had to endure, even though they were in the presence of God and we had never seen God (1 Cor. 6:2). Also, that which tested us here will no longer be able to test us there: Satan and his kingdom will be destroyed (compare 1 Peter 5:8 and Rev. 20:10).

79 Ladd, *The Gospel of the Kingdom*, 95, 106.

80 "[W]here there is no law, there is also no violation" (Rom. 4:15); "sin is not imputed when there is no law" (Rom. 5:13). If there is no higher moral authority than our own human system of right and wrong, fickle and fluid as this might be, then there is nothing to worry about after death. There would be no reckoning, no judgment, and not even any consciousness. Guilt and shame are meaningless; right and wrong are fictitious. But, intuitively, hardly anyone believes this. And despite all resistance of God and His word in this world, it seems that most people do believe in a higher authority. We just may disagree over what (or who) this authority is and how that affects us both now and in a future existence.

81 Ladd, *The Gospel of the Kingdom*, 55.

82 On this point, I strongly recommend my book, *This World Is Not Your Home* (Spiritbuilding Publishing, 2021), in which I dive much deeper into the ongoing spiritual battle between "the darkness" and "the Light"; go to www.spiritbuilding.com/chad.

83 G. E. Ladd, *Jesus and the Kingdom*, quoted in I. H. Marshall, "Kingdom of God," *Zondervan*, 805.

84 JFB, on Mat. 5:3.

85 It is thought that "ten" represents the full number of fingers and thumbs of any given man, to symbolize the perfected or completed work among men. It is not necessarily a work *of* men but a work *concerning* them.

86 Another way of viewing this is that the first seven Beatitudes

speak to the heart, character, and spiritual disposition of kingdom citizens—"seven" symbolizing a holy union between God and people, or the work of God within or through the work of His people. The eighth Beatitude (concerning persecution) symbolizes a new development of such citizens: because they have embraced the seven, therefore they will experience the eighth. Persecution, when it comes (and Jesus virtually promises that it will), is dependent upon one's practice of the first seven Beatitudes. Otherwise, he is being persecuted for something less or other than the kingdom of God, which is a pointless suffering.

87   "Though the full realization of the salvation promised to the poor in spirit may be something of the future according to the rest of the Beatitudes, this nonetheless does not mean that its blessing must be conceived as something that cannot be given and received in the present" (Ridderbos, 78).

88   Strong, G1377.

89   John Bright, *The Kingdom of God* (Nashville, TN: Abingdon Press, 1981), 96.

90   The comparison to David killing Goliath should not be lost on us here. With a single stone, David toppled and executed a giant and set in motion a dynastic kingdom that, through Christ's reign, would never end.

91   Chad Sychtysz, *1 Corinthians Quick Study Commentary* (Spiritbuilding Publishers, 2024), 100–106.

92   This helps us to understand "the law of Christ" (Gal. 6:2). This "law" is not merely commandments and obligations that we are to keep (but these, too, as evidenced in Gal. 6:1–2) but is the guiding principle, the binding element, and the finest virtue among God's people (Col. 3:14).

93   O. Palmer Robertson, quoted in Perrin, 58.

94   Gordon Hugenberger, quoted in Perrin, 58.

95   Bright, 65.

96   Ladd, "Kingdom of God," *ISBE*.

97   Lloyd-Jones, 160–6.

98   Humphreys, *Holman* (electronic).

99 Thayer, G932.

100 Albert Barnes, *Barnes' Notes on the New Testament*, electronic edition (database © 2014 by WORDsearch Corp.), on Mat. 6:33.

101 Ladd, *The Gospel of the Kingdom*, 21.

102 Lloyd-Jones, 147.

103 Jesus' own disciples were shocked when He referred to the Pharisees as blind guides and plants that the Father did not plant (Mat. 15:12–14). No doubt many Jews struggled with Jesus' characterization of the Pharisees as those who played the part of pious believers but inwardly were "full of dead men's bones and all uncleanness" (see Mat. 23:13–27).

104 Ladd, *The Gospel of the Kingdom*, 79.

105 To "deny" oneself necessarily involves repentance of whatever stands opposed to God. Gratifying the flesh, indulging in ungodly behavior, insisting on one's own way, etc., all must be surrendered in this denial. No one can "come after" Christ who refuses to deny his own will, because human desire and God's will are at odds with each other (Gal. 5:16–17).

106 Ladd, *The Gospel of the Kingdom*, 97.

107 Bright, 154; bracketed words are mine.

108 See Mat. 23:5. A phylactery was a very small box that was strapped to one's forehead or on one's forearm and contained excerpts of Scripture. Among the Jews, it was a literal manifestation of what Moses meant to be a spiritual practice (see Deut. 6:8 and 11:18). Some Jews still wear these today.

109 Shurer, 2nd div., 2:131–132.

110 For a positive usage, see Mat. 25:34. For a negative usage, which is more common, see 1 Cor. 6:9–10, 15:50, Gal. 5:21, and Eph. 5:5.

111 The exception would be if there was no son; see Num. 36 and Josh. 17:3–6.

112 This recalls what I said earlier about whether human souls can sin in heaven. I maintain that they cannot, since sin is associated with death, and death is the result of sin. If there is no death in heaven, then neither

can there be sin. And if there is no sin, there is no need for mercy, grace, or forgiveness. These are actions required to remedy sin and have no need to be imparted where there is no sin. I realize Paul said, "sin is not imputed when there is no law" (Rom. 5:13), making it seem as if heaven must be a lawless existence for it to be a sinless one. But this is not accurate. Laws are for people who need to learn about who God is, what must be done (or avoided) to have fellowship with Him, and how sin must be atoned (consider Gal. 3:19, 24, 1 Tim. 1:8–11, and Heb. 10:1–3, all in principle). In heaven, we will see God face to face, we will already have proved our devotion to Him (in this life), and we will never choose to disobey Him because we will be completely and eternally content with and fulfilled by Him in every sense. While there are many other things to consider regarding this topic, this is what I understand the situation to be in the hereafter for God's people.

www.ingramcontent.com/pod-product-compliance
Lightning Source LLC
Chambersburg PA
CBHW050030090426
42735CB00021B/3429